RACHEL, THE 'WRITE' TO SPEAK

Sandra Capelin

MINERVA PRESS

LONDON

MONTREUX WASHINGTON SYDNEY

RACHEL, THE 'WRITE' TO SPEAK
Copyright © Sandra Capelin 1997

ISBN 1 86106 634 1

First Published 1997 by
MINERVA PRESS
195 Knightsbridge
London SW7 1RE

Printed in Great Britain for Minerva Press

RACHEL, THE 'WRITE' TO SPEAK

Please note: some names in this book have
been altered to protect identity.

For Philip and Rachel
without whom this book could not have been written,

and

Thanks to Lorna
for her continual support and encouragement.

AFASIC, which has supported this publication, was founded in 1968 and promotes understanding, acceptance, equal opportunities and the integration into society of children and young adults with speech and language impairments.

Such difficulties range from articulation difficulties to the inability to use or understand language. They may be specific or related to physical disabilities or general learning difficulties.

AFASIC runs a helpline; provides literature and training for both parents and professionals; organises outdoor and arts and drama activities for children and young people; has up to fifty local groups throughout the UK; raises awareness of speech and language impairments and supports the development of local services.

Preface

It is my eternal hope that this book will be of help to many different people. Those who have had to battle to gain recognition for their children's problems may find it easiest to identify with, but I hope it will also encourage others, who have not yet begun a battle but feel there may be one to be fought, to do whatever they feel is instinctively right for their child.

When we have children we often formulate some ideas regarding their future, which usually includes success, intelligence and material gain, but one thing I've learnt as a parent is to modify those aims into health, happiness and satisfaction in knowing that they've done their best for themselves and others.

In some ways I can see that my life had prepared me to cope with Rachel's problems and I have gone on since to help others with similar problems both socially and in my work, which is why I felt this book needed to be written.

Although Phil has not actively written this book he has been closely involved in all the events described. He has also shared in the same feelings and a need to fight for Rachel, so gave me the time to teach her, attend meetings, etc. by carrying the weight of household duties whenever the need arose.

I am proud to be Rachel's mother and to have witnessed her triumph over her difficulties but even more so knowing that she has now opened the door for others.

Contents

Chapter One

We Have a Daughter

Sixteen dirty nappies a day, feeding every hour and nothing but constant screaming! And this was the baby we'd longed and planned for. Why on earth had we bothered?

We had always dreamt of having two children; first a boy and then a little girl so, with Gary being such an easy baby it seemed only natural to have our second child when he was just nineteen months old. After all, I was an experienced sick children's nurse who was used to coping with a ward full of other people's children, so I felt quite confident that I'd be able to cope with my own two offspring!

It all began at 3.15 a.m. on a fine April morning in 1972, when I woke up with what I thought was an awful stomach ache requiring nothing more than a trip to the loo! However, I soon realised how wrong I was halfway down the stairs, so I called for my husband Phil to help me back to bed and then sent him running off to the phone box to let the hospital know we were coming, fetch my parents from across the road to babysit for Gary and to borrow their car, as I knew I couldn't wait for an ambulance. Things were happening too fast! When he returned from his quick sprint around the block, the poor chap set off again to summon an ambulance urgently as it had become apparent that I was in no state to travel by car! Whilst I lay there on my own in heavy labour, intermittently biting my pillow and reassuring Gary that Mummy had only cried out because she'd had a bad dream, I also reflected upon how ironic life was as I had come across so many articles on emergency childbirth during this pregnancy. Strangely enough my mind was so busy coping with the situation that I didn't feel a bit worried or anxious. Instead I kept telling myself that everything must be proceeding normally to happen so fast, as complications would only slow things down, I just lay there giving instructions to my little crew of amateur midwives as they arrived and trusted in God. My father was assigned to Gary whom he soon settled and then no doubt went downstairs to make himself a cup of tea or to do the traditional pacing of floors; my mother took it upon herself to reassure me that nothing would happen just yet but soon agreed with me that the head was coming, after a quick glance in the right direction! I was more than grateful that Phil had been with me for Gary's birth and therefore knew how to support my legs, which my mother then ably assisted with. It wasn't long before our baby dutifully arrived and my mother told me that we had our longed-for daughter. By now it was 3.40 a.m. – everything had happened in less than thirty minutes. It all seemed too good to be true!

Personally, I still felt some clinical responsibility for the situation as I was aware that Rachel (the name we had planned to use for a girl) hadn't given the lusty cry which was needed to enable her breathing mechanism to switch over properly from maternal to independent gear. In fact, her breathing was very shallow but I still didn't panic; instead, my training came to the fore again as I began to stimulate her by rubbing her back and tickling the soles of her feet, after which she gave the most lusty cry and failed to stop!

There was now a dilemma as to what to do about the cord which needed to be cut but I felt confident in waiting for a quarter of an hour. Even so, as no one had arrived from the medical world as yet, I sent my team running to boil our first drop of the traditional gallons of water that are usually required at these events. I suggested that they sterilised some clean string and a sharp pair of scissors whilst I prayed that all would go well; at the same time consoling myself that there wasn't much that could go wrong provided that I tied everything tightly enough!

Thankfully the ambulance team chose that moment to arrive. They summoned a midwife and doctor to come post-haste over their telecom system, which they did, whilst we all relaxed – leaving them to finish off the necessary details.

The first thing the efficient midwife did after cutting the cord was to point out to us that we had left the bedroom window open! None of us had noticed this, so since being thrust from a warm womb at record speed Rachel had been merely wrapped in a towel and gradually allowed to cool off. I felt devastated – how could we have all been so preoccupied that we couldn't think of such a basic thing? Consequently to add to my pique, she dressed Rachel, laid her in a warmed carrycot and promptly took her downstairs to be near the fire as we didn't have central heating in those days. Meanwhile, after I'd washed and been settled in a freshly-made bed I was given two sleeping tablets and told to sleep whilst the rest of the family went downstairs with Rachel, who was still complaining at the top of her newly found voice. Before leaving, the midwife left instructions to feed Rachel with some sugar water at 5 a.m. if she still hadn't stopped crying, but just as they were about to prepare a bottle she stopped and went to sleep.

Of course, I was far too excited to sleep after all that had happened that night. Now that we had our new baby daughter I felt our family was complete – just as we'd always dreamt it would be. As the day began to dawn I decided to slip downstairs to have a peep at Rachel. After all I hadn't even held her yet!

I was to think back on these events many times in the next few years and often wondered if any of it was related to her future problems. She'd been thrust into the world at speed, she hadn't breathed properly for the first one or two minutes and I'd not been allowed to hold her for the first six hours.

Later in the day I tried to breastfeed Rachel but didn't expect to experience any problems. I thought she took the feed well, after which we held her for a while before settling her in her cot. She slept for about twenty minutes but after that she would not be pacified! In the end I tried feeding her again – after all a lot of people believed in demand feeding! After a few days I found I was having to feed her hourly in order to keep her from screaming. It seemed she was only quiet and happy for about twenty minutes following each feed. You could set a clock by it. We didn't know it at the time but this was to become Rachel's style of living for some time to come. Not only that – she had very loose and frequent stools. One day I counted as many as sixteen dirty nappies! The frustrating thing was that nobody really listened or believed in what I was trying to tell them. The midwife just suggested that I drank some whisky following the 6 p.m. feed in the hope of passing it on to Rachel at the 10 p.m. one. Now I hate whisky but I cringed and drank it. I was ready to try anything in order to get some sleep and have a break from that eternal crying. What was I doing wrong? I'd had plenty of experience with children and I'd coped with Gary okay. I'd tried every trick in the book but all the midwife and health visitor could suggest was to try again! My energy was being sapped and I was running out of patience – fast. I was beginning to feel desperate as nothing seemed to pacify her.

When Rachel was ten days old we found that she'd lost two and a quarter pounds in weight. By now I felt quite anxious as I could almost see her 'shrinking' before my eyes but no one else seemed perturbed by this. They merely said she must be allergic to my breast milk so I should try bottle-feeding her. I must admit that this did improve things slightly, in as much as she began to gain weight and I didn't have to feed her so often, but she still cried and screamed an awful lot! My mother seemed to think I'd find it comforting to know that I was considered a bad-tempered child until I was two years old, so she told me so at frequent intervals. It didn't help. I only found it irritating.

One day when I was in the chemist I noticed a product called Sister Laura's something or other, which was supposed to be added to feeds to thicken them and make them easier to digest. I thought anything was worth trying so I bought some. I don't know who Sister Laura was but I will be eternally grateful to her! At three months old Rachel began to settle onto four-hourly feeds and even went through the night. It was a magic formula all right.

It was also about this time that I noticed a difference when holding Rachel in my arms. Up until then I had felt something was missing between us. It's hard to put into words but although I loved her, she didn't seem to respond and snuggle into my arms, moulding herself to me as most babies did. Instead she seemed to remain aloof, almost detached from us. Phil and I both noticed the difference in her but there was still something else that puzzled me about Rachel.

Now I'm afraid I need to be technical for a minute and explain that all babies are born with several reflex reactions, which are all basically concerned with survival, such as sucking when something is put to their mouth. Obviously this reflex lasts for some time but the others usually disappear after a few months as the baby begins to 'suss the joint out' and decides for itself what to do. One of these reflexes is known as the Moro reflex and is probably named after some clever professor who first wrote about it – even though the cavemen's babies certainly had it! It is best described as a reaction to shock as the baby throws its arms out above its head if it feels any sudden change in its position or environment (like being dropped), or as a reaction to sudden loud noise. This reflex has usually disappeared after three months as the baby becomes more aware of its surroundings and begins to assess each situation separately. For some reason or other Rachel continued to react like this to loud noises, especially motorbikes, until she was about eighteen months old! If she was lying in her pram when a motorbike passed by, not only did she throw out her arms with her head thrust back but she would also 'jump' so much that she would visibly leave the mattress! I hated to see her so nervous whilst being totally unable to help her. I felt so inadequate as I could only comfort her afterwards.

I was also aware by now that she would only settle for sleep if she was wrapped tightly in a shawl, like the old-fashioned swaddling clothes. I suppose this helped her to feel safe, as if she was still in the womb. Although I knew something was different about Rachel, I didn't think it was worth making a fuss at this stage.

Eventually we all settled into something of a routine although there were times when I felt I could cheerfully throw her out of the nearest window! (And it was usually an upstairs one that I had in mind too.) There were times when I think I would have lost my nerve if it hadn't been for Gary being such an easy child. I consoled myself with the fact that I'd coped okay with him and I was doing all the same things with her, plus drawing on all my resources gained from my training. I really didn't think I was causing her problems – but I found I questioned myself frequently.

As she grew, so her feeds grew bigger until she was taking nearly a full bottle every four hours. At various intervals I'd tried introducing solid foods but although she took them with relish she always ended up screaming about twenty minutes later. We were back to the old feeding problem in a different guise. I'm afraid I simply postponed facing the ultimate event and told myself that my parents' generation had only been fed on milk until they were six months old and they'd all survived okay. Maybe she had an immature digestive system, I thought, that would eventually right itself given time. It was no good talking to anyone at the clinic as they only suggested everything I'd already tried. After all, it wasn't so long ago that I'd been a nurse handing out the self-same advice! However, when I told them that I'd already tried that little trick I was simply told to go away and try again! Didn't they realise that I was asking for help because I needed some support, even if they couldn't find a cure? I did not want to be placated and merely sent home again!

We carried on in this vein until she was taking a full bottle every four hours, but of course the inevitable had to occur – she started demanding more food. I therefore started to feed her three-hourly which she seemed to find satisfying but I knew it was wrong. By now I'd tried just about every type of reliable starter baby foods and cereals but they all produced the same screaming reaction. In desperation I decided to try her on some powdered adult breakfast cereal and thank goodness we had a contented baby who waited until the next feed. Later, I offered her some breakfast biscuits mashed in milk with the same successful result. I decided there and then to purée all our own suitable foods for her, rather than use any commercial products, which worked extremely well until she was able to eat the usual toddler diet and ultimately a normal diet.

Another problem with Rachel was that she seemed to need an awful lot of entertaining, stimulating and reassurance throughout the day. Unless I could keep her occupied she'd cry. Phil built her a mobile to stand over her carrycot, from which he suspended lots of strings, so that I could tie a different selection of objects on it to keep her amused. I used everything I could think of from toys to milk bottle tops and a colourful plastic tea strainer. As she grew older it seemed she had to be able to see me or she'd cry. I got to one stage when I'd wake up in the morning to feed her, then after washing and dressing her I'd just shut her in her room until I'd completed all the essential morning tasks, including preparing the dinner, so that I'd only got to switch on the gas at the required time. I got this down to about half an hour's work as I charged around like greased lightning! I felt guilty hearing her wailing away upstairs but it was the only way I could cope with her and the housework. After I'd finished we'd all go out for a walk to the shops so that we could both calm down. Fortunately Gary seemed oblivious to all this and just seemed to accept that babies generally cried a lot anyhow. For the rest of the day I'd carry her about or keep her with me, somehow doing most things one-handed until Phil came home.

My mother continued to reassure me that I'd been a bad-tempered baby until I was two years old but I still didn't find this news very helpful, though I did pray that Rachel would miraculously reach that magical age soon! Later, when she could sit up, I would try sitting her in her playpen surrounded by toys whilst doing some chores, but she would start crying every time I passed by if I didn't stop and stay with her. On these occasions I worked out a strategy whereby, if she was happily amusing herself for five minutes, I would sneak out of the back door and in through the front door rather than risk going through the lounge and create another bawling match. I could not believe that I'd sunk to such depths of inadequacy. I was a trained children's nurse and already a mother of one child. Why couldn't I cope with this one?

When she was six months old I was offered an appointment to see a paediatrician. This was really arranged because of my complaints about her previous difficulties with solids, but I decided to use it to discuss everything else and was duly advised by this eminent, professional consultant that I had a bad-tempered baby. He said I had to control her now or she would soon learn to control me. I found this piece of advice just about as useful as my mother's little well-worn phrase!

Chapter Two

The Early Years

Both children continued to develop normally and seemed to reach their necessary milestones at the right times. Gary had continual ear infections and a few other interesting health problems along the way, but always remained a very placid and amiable chap. He needed to be, with his sister as she was! He also loved language and was extremely articulate and chatty. As he obviously enjoyed playing with multi-syllable words I consciously tried to introduce a new one into our conversation each week. Consequently, by the time he went to playschool he was already discussing things like the rain cycle and evaporation, simply because he found them interesting subjects.

Gary was also a natural pacifist so did nothing to protect himself or his rights, but he was a fierce defender of his little sister if anyone tried to hurt her! She, however, was remarkably healthy but still continued to be bad-tempered – screaming and throwing frequent tantrums for no apparent reason. By now I was beginning to console myself with my mother's well-known phrase or saying, "Well, you were a bad-tempered child till you were two years old," and I gave up going to the clinic as I only felt frustrated when they were unable to help me. When Rachel reached that long-awaited age of two years, she began to take an interest in picture books but for some reason she always held the book upside down! Even when we corrected her she would reverse it again, as if to say, "this is the way I see it best, thank you very much!" Although her language seemed to develop at a reasonable rate I did notice that she had a good vocabulary but didn't always use the words in the right places, but I thought this was just immature speech which would eventually right itself. After all, Gary had been advanced in speech but slower to walk whereas Rachel had launched herself at ten months but was slower to talk. When Gary entered full-time school he was already beginning to read and took to school like a duck to water. I therefore had more time to observe Rachel; but the more I noticed the more puzzled I became! For one thing I became a regular helper at playschool and noticed that although Rachel loved to do jigsaws or sticking if personally guided by an assistant, she generally preferred to just run round and round the large apparatus if left to her own devices, occasionally going on the slide or some such piece, but then proceeding to charge around like a lunatic again.

I was intrigued by her choice of friends too, as she always seemed to gravitate towards the children who were younger than her or those who were generally described as being odd and would probably end up at special schools. However, I did nothing to stop this as I felt it was important for Rachel to develop some friendships of her own. Even at home, she didn't seem to want to play with toys and lacked any imaginative play, so I still found her very difficult to keep amused.

By the time she was four years old I thought it was time she knew her colours, but despite all our efforts she still continued to use any old colour name when she felt a label was required. I therefore decided to sit down with her one day when we were alone and try to see whether or not she was colour-blind. I got together lots of bricks and various other red, blue, yellow and green objects in subtle shades to see if she could group them. I reckon she could have done it standing on her head! She had no problem at all. It was obvious then that it was the labelling process that was causing her difficulties.

After that I started to become aware of all the other oddities in her language. Unlike Gary's love of new words being introduced into his vocabulary, she would flatly refuse to try to repeat a new word. Sometimes if we tried to show something to Rachel, thinking she would like to see it, she would close her eyes refusing to look and say, "I can't see it!" Another little trick she developed was to avoid describing things by always showing us or demonstrating, tending to point and say, "there", "that", "this one" or "those" rather than use a noun (naming word), adjective (describing word) or preposition (position word). She also confused such words as "eat" and "drink" or "hot" and "cold".

One day when visiting a travelling fairground for a family outing she indicated that she would like a toffee apple but insisted on purchasing it for herself. Unfortunately this resulted in bitter tears because Rachel actually asked the stall holder for some candy floss, which of course she gave her.

Any attempts to correct Rachel's errors would result in tantrums so we tended to just repeat correctly what we thought she meant. Sometimes this also caused a scene if she insisted on using *her* word but we got by, as long as we did the right thing and *not* necessarily what she'd said! Very confusing at times as can be imagined. I'm afraid it all became a matter of compromise in an attempt to avoid any unnecessary frustration tantrums.

It was about now that my mother began to acknowledge that Rachel might be more difficult than I had been! Actually, my nerves and stamina were being stretched to their limits. It was taking all my strength to stay in charge of the situation and I was secretly beginning to wonder how long I would be able to control her. Even if I succeeded when she was aged four years, I dreaded to think what she'd be like as a teenager!

One of her least endearing ways was the way in which she found a hundred and one ways of saying the same thing over and over again. This was particularly difficult to cope with at about 5 a.m. when we were hoping for a lie-in! She would start off by calling out all our names and telling us individually that she was awake. As if we hadn't noticed! She'd then go on to say, "I'm not asleep. Are you asleep, Gary?" and work her way through each of us again. And so it went on until either Phil or I ended up telling her – in no uncertain terms – to be quiet! This never lasted for long though as she couldn't amuse herself and craved for companionship and entertainment. She still needed constant company when awake and unfortunately for us she needed very little sleep.

One of the most difficult things to cope with for both Rachel and us was her absolute fear of anything she could not understand, or which she thought was beyond her control. The world must have been a very confusing place for her as she needed to trust both the people close to her and the actual objects around her in order to feel safe. She loved her inflatable Mickey Mouse, which had always been fully inflated ready for play since her first birthday, until one day it developed a puncture. When she realised its size and shape had changed she wouldn't go near it – not even after Phil had repaired the puncture and blown it up again. As she couldn't understand what had happened, she wouldn't trust it any more. Any attempts to bring it near her resulted in real terror so it was given away. After that, all inflatable objects such as the children's paddling pool were treated with the same distrust.

Another real fear was the sand, which was a shame as we lived near the beach. I can only assume that she felt insecure on the sand as it didn't feel as solid as the earth surface which she was used to standing on in the garden or on the pavements. As a baby we left her in her pushchair, then gradually progressed to sitting on a blanket, eventually she ventured onto the sand wearing shoes and by the time she was five years old she played on the firmer wet sand in bare feet, gradually progressing to the drier stuff as her confidence grew. This was relatively easy to cope with compared with moving water, such as rivers or the sea. That took the patience of a saint to deal with – and a saint with earmuffs too!

Sudden loud noises still remained a problem as well. Whenever an aeroplane flew over, no matter how high in the sky, Rachel would run indoors, and motorbikes proved a constant problem as they were always there on the roads as we tried to walk along the pavements. If she came remotely near a motorbike, either on the road or in the display window of a garage or shop, she'd freeze and go ramrod stiff. The only way we could pass was by carrying her, which was not easy when she was so stiff that she couldn't bend. This problem was compounded by the fact that a crash helmet represented a motorbike to her – after all she didn't know which bit might suddenly make that awful noise. Her own grandfather rode a motorbike but she couldn't bring herself to enter their lounge if his crash helmet was on the table. Also if he came into the room carrying it she would hide behind a chair. She was absolutely petrified.

Father Christmas became a phobia to such an extent that he had to be sent a note asking him to leave any toys or presents for our house in the shed, before she would relax enough to go to sleep. She wasn't having any strange man coming down her chimney in the middle of the night! We did try warning her playgroup leader prior to the Christmas party but I think she felt she would cope okay as many of the children were either shy or anxious about that strange man who just seemed to appear annually. I don't think she quite expected the amount of real panic that set in, though.

It took us years of effort and patience to gradually desensitise her from each thing individually but I'm afraid a lot of it had to wait until she was about eight years old when her language and reasoning ability had improved enough for her to have a better understanding of the world in general.

Unfortunately it was about this time that her eating habits became a major issue yet again. Following the age-old advice, I started off by ignoring it but soon realised that if Rachel had her way she would only eat her pudding but no dinner and only cake for tea, having ignored her first course. Breakfast was the only meal she would eat properly. I then decided to start saying, "Well, if you can't eat your dinner you can't be very hungry, so there's no pudding," and used the same policy at tea-time, but I soon realised that she was as strong as me, so she ended up by going without! I thought hunger would be bound to win over in the end. I even stopped giving her milk and biscuits in between meals so that she just drank water. We didn't make an issue of it or even try to discuss it with her; we just quietly removed her plate and waited until the next meal. This went on for a fortnight, after which I began to worry. I was afraid that her health would begin to suffer if I let her carry on like that, so decided to give her the most minuscule meal of a teaspoonful of mince, a teaspoonful of mashed potato, one piece of diced carrot and one pea and then insisted that she ate it all, which could take her up to two hours.

I must admit that I sometimes resorted to force-feeding her but then she only ran up to the front door or into the toilet to make herself sick, after which I'd feed her again. Now this did upset Gary. He'd coped admirably with all her frustration and temper tantrums. He didn't resent all the extra attention she seemed to get at such times as I always made a point of talking it through with him afterwards and trying to give him some extra time as well but he hated seeing me being forceful with her. I hated it too but I was so worried that her stomach was beginning to adjust to just one meal a day. This pattern did eventually break but only after many battles and lots of heartbreak and tears from both of us. She was so strong-willed but I felt it would be detrimental to her both physically and mentally to let her win this particular battle. Rachel remained a difficult eater until she was about eight years old but many years later, I learnt that not only did she have an orthodontic problem but that children with her problems often have eating difficulties as well! However, at that time all I knew was that I had a difficult child to deal with, and according to the paediatrician I was supposed to win.

Chapter Three

School Begins

When Rachel began full-time school I felt she wasn't really ready to start formal education but knew that all the children would be at different levels of readiness, so I hoped that she'd be able to fit in somewhere. After all, she was keen to start and that was the main thing; she thought she'd be clever like Gary now and learn to read and write too. In order to prepare her we had taken her along to all the big school functions, such as concerts and sports days, and she'd seen all the children milling around in the playground, so there was no fear of the unknown in that area. It was a small school, consisting of three classes with thirteen children in the reception class, so I just braced myself and hoped that she would soon settle in and start learning to do whatever was expected of her.

The first day went reasonably well but her teacher did tell me that Rachel had refused to draw a picture when asked. Oh dear, I knew she was strong-minded but I hadn't imagined she'd be that strong-willed in such a setting! On reflection I could see that Rachel was only trying to protect herself from humiliation, but unfortunately her teacher hadn't realised this; kind though this lady was. Have you ever tried explaining such a thing to your child's teacher? How often are we, the parents (who are, after all, supposed to know our children best) labelled as being overprotective, over-aspiring or fussy parents if we dare try to explain our child's point of view? Well, I didn't want that to happen on her first day, so I just reiterated the expected phrase and told Rachel that she should have tried to do as asked.

Apparently all the new children had been asked to draw a picture of themselves but I can imagine Rachel's heart sank at such a request as her drawings were still very primitive and she could only draw a 'stick' person. She therefore decided to play safe by drawing a picture of her house instead but of course it was a typical, primitive type house and the teacher was not too pleased! When she had reminded Rachel of what she was supposed to have drawn and sent her back to do just that, Rachel had known it was beyond her ability so had refused. Not a good start!

As time went on we, couldn't see any real change in her from playschool. She still drew all her pictures on the back of cards or project folders and she still wrote her name back to front as in mirror writing. She was also slow to learn to read.

We went along to the first parents' evening hoping to discuss our daughter's intriguing little enigmas. I was sure that something was not quite right as she seemed so bright in many ways and was more alert than Gary at times. We looked at all the children's paintings displayed on the wall accompanied by their writing, but Rachel's just consisted of a painted blue blob on a large piece of paper with what appeared to be an "a", "c", and "t" arranged haphazardly around the blob. (It seemed this was her total writing skill developed after one term at school.) Under her painting the teacher had written, "This is Rachel's Daddy's car". She was the only one who hadn't done her own writing and we hadn't been able to recognise her attempt of our car, even though we knew it was blue! When we asked the teacher what she felt was causing Rachel's problems she simply described her as a highly-strung child who was taking longer than usual to settle in. It seemed she was constantly running into the adjoining classroom to see her brother as well.

However, when it came to the school's Christmas concert Rachel was in her element and excelled herself by taking the part of Little Miss Muffet and singing a solo verse whilst alone on stage. She knew the nursery rhyme well and was full of confidence in situations like this. What a complex creature she was!

Rachel's fears and frustrations continued to cause us problems and if anything the temper tantrums were becoming stronger and longer. Very often she would try to tell us something but we'd misunderstand; such situations would immediately be followed by, "You don't know what I mean!", after which she would burst into tears and sob – sometimes for as long as twenty minutes. I found it best on these occasions, to just sit on the floor with her on my lap, hold her tight and rock back and forth until the storm abated. Then we would try again to gently work out what she was trying to say. Sometimes there was no containing her though, and she would simply lie on the floor thrashing her arms and legs about until she finally exhausted herself. Interestingly Rachel kept these exhibitions of frustration private, so my mother and others found it hard to believe that she could behave in this way, until they experienced it for themselves.

One day my mother was trying to explain how to play a simple game of cards to Rachel, but she found it too hard to understand and threw the whole pack of cards at her grandmother – who subsequently discovered how strong Rachel was whilst trying to make her pick them up again! Another time Rachel threw all the cushions from the three-piece suite onto the floor and refused to pick them up. After that my mother began to believe me, but to most other people Rachel portrayed herself as a shy, quiet little 'wallflower' who generally just answered "Yes," "No" or "I don't know," when out of her depth in a conversation, so gave the appearance of not being very bright as well. I knew I was dealing with something beyond my own capabilities and felt frustrated because we could barely cope but *no one* seemed either to listen or believe us.

To say that Rachel was an unreasonable child is a little harsh but the fact remains that she could not be reasoned with. She often appeared to listen to an explanation as to why she couldn't do something but always answered with the same response, "I know but I want to!"

One of the few things that Rachel did find enjoyable was dancing, as she had always enjoyed moving to music since a very early age. Initially she began with an unambitious group who simply danced for pleasure and produced the occasional show but, in spite of her difficulties, Rachel set herself high standards and quickly wanted to move on to a dancing school that used barres and spoke French. Goodness knows why, when she found English so hard, but I think she had been inspired by a romantic children's series on television, which had revolved around a girl at ballet school. I found it very difficult to find a sympathetic teacher in the district who had high standards but didn't push pupils through examinations, but eventually I found one in the next town. Luckily, her best friend Heather (who, as usual, was a year younger than Rachel) began at the same time so Rachel had some support for her first visits. This friendship proved to be a long-standing one which was probably reinforced by their mutual love of dancing. Something that both girls still enjoy today.

By the time Rachel had reached six-and-a-half years old I was all but dragging her to school crying every day. Once or twice she even went so far as to complain of a sore throat, so I took her to the doctor, only to discover that she was perfectly all right – just skiving from school! She was then in a top infant class being prepared for junior school, but she was by no means ready for this. Every time I tried to speak to anyone about the problems I thought she had, I was simply told that she was all right; there were plenty of children like Rachel in school. I felt patronised. Maybe there were plenty with her degree of ability but were they all as upset by their lack of achievement? How many others were being dragged to school crying each day and generally getting into such frustration tantrums? Anyway they were *their* parents' problems and Rachel was ours – to cope with alone it seemed from the amount of support being offered!

Even Rachel's play seemed different from other children's. She appeared to be fixed on playing Mummies and Daddies, which simply meant acting out everyday circumstances; she still showed little imagination in her play and although she was good at doing jigsaws, she was reluctant to play with any other toys. It seemed as though she didn't know *how* to play properly. Later I realised that a good knowledge of language is needed before a child can use it in imaginative play.

I'm afraid mealtimes still remained an on-going problem as she did not appear to enjoy eating. It seemed to have become a matter of principle to us both and had now developed – rightly or wrongly – into a battle of wills. I often felt guilty but with no professional advice I continued to do what I thought best, which was to stick to our rule of Rachel eating the minuscule meal provided.

Although they were diminishing as her understanding grew, a lot of her fears and phobias were still present, accompanied by an extraordinary degree of fear in any new situation. Sometimes she even lacked confidence in people that we thought she trusted, like the family of her other close friend Linda, who lived a few doors away from us. Now Linda and Rachel practically lived together, eating and playing in each other's houses and Linda often slept with us but Rachel could not bring herself to sleep in Linda's house. One night when this was tried, Rachel went to bed in Linda's house, but left and came home to sleep at about 8.30 p.m., and then went back to Linda's for breakfast! If they invited her to go with them on an outing, Rachel would only go if they took Gary too or if I went as well. She wouldn't even walk the few doors up the street to Linda's house alone.

By now she had somehow managed to achieve a reasonable reading age at school but would still read some words backwards; for example she read "tell" for "let" and "saw" for "was" – but nothing distressed her more than having to write a story. She lived in dread of story-writing each school day and usually only managed to write about three lines, after which she'd print THE END in block capitals as if to say, "that's all I'm doing so don't you think otherwise." It seemed none of her work was ever completed.

On looking in her school books I could see that about half her writing was still mirrored and this extended into her number work as well; she wrote "21" as "12" as well as reversing her number shapes. Consequently a lot of her work was marked wrong when her calculations were in fact correct, which obviously caused her great distress. She knew she had to try hard to improve her "untidy handwriting" as she called it, but to mark her sums wrong when she felt they were right seemed like a gross injustice to her.

I'm afraid her art work was no better as her drawings were still very immature, consisting of either a primitively drawn house or girl and most cards or project folders were still being illustrated on the back. By now, she was beginning to become inhibited in her creative work. I remember one day she came home particularly distressed because she was the only one in the class not to have a project folder. Apparently the whole class had been growing cress in an egg shell, which Rachel had really enjoyed doing, coming home and telling us little bits about it. When they came to do their writing the teacher had given them a folder to put their work in and asked them to illustrate the front cover; but of course, Rachel drew her picture on the back. The teacher took it away and placed another folder in front of her the correct way round but Rachel promptly turned it over and drew on the back again. The teacher told me she did this three times, after which she felt Rachel was being deliberately obstinate, so she refused to give her a fourth folder.

I think the more that was asked of Rachel in school, the more she failed, and like the first day at school she tried to avoid such humiliation. If she'd had the courage I think she might have opted out but luckily, she was blessed with great determination and a strong desire to succeed instead.

I noticed at home that she was quite a clumsy child; often spilling the milk when pouring it over her cereal in the morning, unless I put the milk in a small cream jug to save her yet another embarrassing failure. She was also useless at ball games – preferring to duck rather than try to catch a ball, no matter how large or small or how near or gently thrown to her. She couldn't skip with a skipping rope either and although she loved dancing she had great difficulty in remembering a simple sequence of steps. I really don't know how she coped with her dancing as she couldn't remember and repeat a rhythm when clapping and I was convinced by her singing at this stage that she must be tone-deaf!

Her language was still not developing as we'd hoped either. Most people thought she was just shy because of the way she avoided entering into conversations with others or just gave very brief or simple answers. She had, however, grown into quite a pretty girl and had discovered that she could often get by quite easily by being coy with men! Those eyes could be quite amazing at times!

At home she spoke quite freely but her words were often muddled and swapped around, or else she'd substitute words with something similar such as calling Girl Guides "blue Brownies" and hearing aids "deaf boxes". Sometimes she would say something completely bizarre like, "I've swutched the rectangle on" which meant, "I've switched the radio on". Whenever we tried to talk or explain something to her she'd simply walk off whilst we were in mid-sentence or go completely 'loony' and act like a stupid little idiot, going all giggly and behaving in a most ridiculous fashion so that the conversation came to a standstill.

Now it seems amazing to look back on all this and to realise that we had just let things ride along at their own pace for so long but I had been told so many times by my GP, paediatricians, teachers and even friends that they felt there was nothing wrong with Rachel. They all said she was no different from many other children, she was just bad-tempered and strong-willed and I was constantly reminded that we all muddled our words at times.

Simultaneously to this I was also having to cope with Gary's various ailments which included being investigated at different times for TB and even cancer, along with his fortnightly ear infections (nine of which perforated his ear drums) and excessive bruising for minor injuries. The school and his cub leaders were asking us the same questions that we were asking the doctors regarding the bruising but our GP simply dismissed it as being boyish 'war wounds' whilst casualty questioned *us* for physical child abuse! Several years later when Gary was twelve years old we discovered that he had been born with haemophilia, but that was only after he'd bled excessively at home and taken nearly a month to heal following some minor dental extractions to help straighten his teeth.

Perhaps now you can imagine how I was beginning to feel. I was constantly questioning my own gut feelings and beliefs and began to think that I was the one with a problem – not my children! I therefore tried to believe all these other people and to accept Gary and Rachel as they were and told myself that I was becoming neurotic.

However, deep down I knew this was not true. I knew in my heart that Rachel definitely had a problem but no one else seemed to believe me. At times I tried to explain things to my sister who always listened, but I knew she was at a loss when it came to helping me, apart from allowing me to cry out my frustrations on her shoulder, which helped me a great deal but didn't change a thing for Rachel. My poor sister had always looked upon me as the expert in the family when it came to child-rearing but there I was, blatantly not coping with my own! One thing she had noticed though, was that I seemed to treat Gary and Rachel differently when disciplining them – not that Gary needed much correction as he always responded to a reasonable explanation but I was very aware that whenever Rachel threw one of her tantrums or began sobbing, I felt myself literally switch into what I can only describe as a 'clinical gear' emotionally. I remember thinking, "Here we go again" and physically feeling a change in my attitude, but if I'd remained in my normal gear, I think I'd have joined in rather than cope with her problems.

I always felt that no one could really have as many problems in life as Rachel seemed to have, so one day I decided to sit down and tried to catalogue everything, listing all her problems from birth to the present day in order to help me understand what exactly I was dealing with. Surely all these things stemmed from one basic problem, if only we could discover what it was! I continued to keep a monthly record to review her problems and at the same time tried to work out a programme of games and activities to help her.

To begin with I decided to test out her hand and eye co-ordination along with her general physical skills which I knew were poor. We worked hard at hopping, skipping and ball games but at first she couldn't even catch a large beach ball when it was almost placed in her hands. At the slightest hint of a throw from anything more than six inches (fifteen centimetres) away she would duck and shield her face! Gradually, in gentle stages we progressed to using smaller balls, covering larger distances, and eventually moved on to bat and ball games. Although her ability to catch balls made relatively slow progress, I was amazed at how well Rachel responded and how quickly she learnt when we started with the basics and broke everything down into easy stages for her.

I also read as many books on learning difficulties as I could find and understand. Through doing this I came across a few recommended activity books, some of which involved drawing a lot of lines from left to right and tracing. Surprisingly, Rachel did not find these too boring. Instead she seemed to enjoy the challenge and was openly grateful and relieved to know that at least we acknowledged that she did have a problem which we wanted to help her with.

By helping out at a local school and reading lots of library books I had also learnt the importance of body control in large and small motor (physical) activities, but first the child had to really understand its own body and how it related to its surroundings. For example, the child has to know that its head and body are joined by its neck. Lots of children fail to realise this until quite late in their development. The understanding of left and right is also important. Even if the child doesn't know the different names, it needs to decide on a dominant hand and to be able to distinguish between what's on this side of the room and what's on that side. Rachel had no understanding of her left and right and used either hand to point, pick up and even to catch. She had no understanding of how the objects around her related to each other either. For example, she couldn't say "the cup on the table" or understand "under the chair". Now how can a child be expected to learn that "c" is followed by "a" which is followed by "t" to spell "cat" in a left to right pattern if it doesn't really understand left and right? And how can a child learn the positioning of short and tall letters without fully understanding the meaning of under and over?

I therefore began to realise that in order to read, children had to be able to recognise shapes and understand how everyday objects related to each other.

In order to learn this we encouraged her to play with lots of big cardboard boxes in the garden and to climb over all sorts of playground apparatus whilst we talked all the time about "on, under, over, through", etc. Fortunately she enjoyed all these activities, was keen to learn to skip and loved playing hopscotch. She was determined to overcome all her difficulties because she hated to be thought 'stupid' by other children and therefore responded well to all structured teaching. Dancing was also a fun way to reinforce left and right and was good practice for learning sequences and remembering what came next – even if it did entail my going along to the lesson every so often to learn the new dance as well so that I could help her at home. Rachel was so keen that she would then practise at home morning, noon and night until she could do it without my prompting her. It was this degree of determination to succeed that chiefly gave us the strength and motivation to help her, although it was very demanding along with all the other chores and commitments involved in family life.

Chapter Four
Time for Strategies

After Rachel had settled into main school I was lucky enough to secure a job in a hearing impaired unit as a teaching assistant. The work mainly consisted of helping the deaf children when they integrated with the hearing children in the classroom and my experience there was to prove invaluable when helping Rachel. It was whilst working there that I met Julie, a trained speech therapist and teacher of the deaf, who soon became a very good friend, as we discovered that we both had the same sense of humour, held similar views on many different subjects and enjoyed all the same leisure activities. Before working at the unit Julie had been employed at a local school for language-impaired children and both taught and used a variety of sign languages. I found her a fascinating person and we spent many lunch hours discussing all sorts of topics and generally attempting to put the world to rights.

It was whilst talking to Julie that I poured out my feelings, frustrations and confusions about Rachel. I felt encouraged because she was the first person who seemed to really *understand* and *believe* me; not only that, she had met Rachel and knew her to be a bright little girl so therefore didn't try to patronise me.

In fact Julie offered to assess Rachel for me! Now I hadn't been expecting that and felt thrown into confusion but she explained that as part of her training as a speech therapist and a teacher of the deaf she had been taught how to assess a child's language and some other areas of their development. I didn't know what to say. As much as I wanted an assessment done, I didn't want Julie to have the embarrassment of telling a friend that she was neurotic and that her child was fine – as everyone else seemed to think! Julie went on to explain that if we didn't want to accept her offer, we did have the right, as parents, to ask our local educational psychologist Kevin Brown to examine Rachel and that her school couldn't stop us. I felt immediately grateful to Julie for her help but decided to wait and think it over with Phil that night.

That evening we talked at some length but it was not an easy decision to make. Although we felt tempted to accept Julie's offer of help because we knew and trusted her implicitly, we didn't want to put her in a difficult situation. At the same time I knew Kevin Brown to be a well-liked and respected man who worked a lot with our deaf children and often came into the unit. We therefore decided to ask him to do the assessment and wrote a polite letter to Rachel's school to inform them of our decision. That was in March but I knew there was a long waiting list to see Kevin so we decided to continue with our own programme of activities in the meantime.

We had finished the books in which she'd practised tracing from left to right and had moved on to some other remedial activity books, which she seemed to enjoy just as much. Another thing which helped her was the new video game which was becoming a modern craze and involved a game of TV tennis. By sitting on the left of the screen and only controlling the figure on the left-hand side, Rachel had to watch the ball go from left to right. This was supposed to help reinforce the eye movements needed for reading and writing in a fun way. At first she was absolutely useless at it and had no idea of how to use the control but as usual, when taught in a simple structured way, she quickly became quite proficient.

We also joined the toy library to enable us to play with all the different educational toys available in the cheapest possible way. One of the first toys we borrowed was a big wooden posting box which used very specific shapes, such as a cross with two fat and two thin 'arms', which could only be posted in one way. I thought this was ideal to help Rachel learn to recognise the specific direction of shape as she needed to do with letters. Although she found it quite difficult she enjoyed playing with it because she enjoyed the challenge. One day when we had all the pieces spread out over the carpet in the lounge feeling and talking about the different shapes, my mother arrived and walked into the room but immediately started to cry, to see her granddaughter, aged nearly seven years, playing with a baby's toy. I remember I told her to get out if she couldn't cope and not to come back until she'd sorted herself out! I said that if she preferred to see Rachel remain as she was and suffer, she could leave, because I was prepared to do everything necessary to help her.

Needless to say it hurt me too, to find that my daughter still couldn't play with such basic toys competently, but I was glad to find anything suitable which could help her and be used as part of her training. I was also inspired by Rachel's own motivation and the way she learnt so quickly when we used the step-by-step 'touch and feel' method.

We felt it best to leave Rachel to cope with her school work in term time but to continue with our programme of books and games each holiday, in the hope of easing Rachel's problems and frustrations until the educational psychologist could see her. I knew he was very busy and that it would be a long time before her appointment but we were sure it would be worth it in the end – at least we would then have an honest and unbiased opinion at last.

Unfortunately we felt unable to help Rachel with many other problems such as her refusal to participate in any 'learning type' of conversations, the way she muddled her words or couldn't explain things and her unaccountable, amazing fear of unknown situations. I can well remember one trip to a popular picnic area (known locally as 'The Gibbet' due to its past history) where there were some chalk cliffs, down which most children loved to slide, scramble back up and then slide down again. Some brought old tin trays with them specifically for this purpose whilst others simply wore holes in their trousers! We had dressed our children in hardy old playclothes for this trip, as had my sister who went with us, bringing her three-year-old son, Brett. I'm afraid Rachel saw danger in nearly everything Brett did and become so overprotective that I'm surprised the poor little chap didn't lash out at her in frustration! Later we chose to go on a walk along the clifftops, around the perimeter of the area; now that really did panic Rachel. Even my sister was amazed at the degree of Rachel's fear as she had never really witnessed her in such a state before. Not only did she scream and sob most of the way around, she froze to the spot refusing to walk and held herself so ramrod stiff that she couldn't bend – which made it very difficult for Phil to carry her!

Eventually, after about six weeks of the aforementioned holiday activities, we did begin to see some improvement in Rachel. At first we noticed that although her pictures only displayed a basic house and primitive people, she was beginning to add trees and flowers. She still had difficulty in copying some shapes but was beginning to struggle to draw some animals and had made a good attempt at a cat sitting down!

She still didn't finish a picture when colouring but her handwriting was definitely improving, in spite of an incredible lack of finger spaces or word grouping. Rachel was definitely trying to help herself. She had become quite accomplished at using the video game and was now aware of her right hand which she tried hard to use consistently. I even noticed her correcting herself if she used her left hand by mistake. All this again reinforced our belief that we were right to help Rachel and encouraged us to continue with our planned programme in spite of what anyone else thought of us.

It was in late April when we really noticed a big change in her though. One day we were sitting at a table looking at a book together when we came across a picture of some Red Indians complete with head-dress. It was a week before my birthday and she couldn't have given me a better present if she'd spent a million pounds. Rachel actually asked me a question about the Indians! She didn't manage to phrase the question properly but by pointing and the intonation of her voice I could tell that she wanted to know why they wore feathers in their hair. I answered her as simply as I could, as if answering a two-year-old, and she listened and accepted the reply, but chose to end the conversation there. I cannot explain how I felt – I wanted to shout for joy, say a prayer of thanksgiving, go out in the street to dance and hug the first person who came along! All at once if that was possible. Rachel had asked her first question and I was both relieved and delighted even though she was in fact seven years old.

After that she began to query different words which she heard us use in general conversation such as "logical" or "pollution". I don't think she always understood them, even with a simple explanation, but she wasn't put off and continued to ask more questions – even if they confused me at times. I remember one day she asked, "Is Australia in England, Mummy?" I felt ecstatic at the daily changes and improvement we were now seeing in her; it was as though she was really starting to open the door to understanding and learning. Only a few weeks before, I had been in despair because of her totally closed mind but now it was gently opening. It was wonderful to see.

During the Easter holidays she showed a real enthusiasm in helping Phil and Gary to plant the seeds in our back garden. Gary had always taken a great delight in having his own little plot of land since he was a toddler but had now progressed to actually helping with the main crop of vegetables for the family. Rachel had been offered the same experiences but had refused to join in, still, it seemed this year was to be different. Phil was as amazed and excited as me at the way she responded when shown the seeds. In fact he said she went on to look around to find some more; she also maintained an interest when he asked her, "How many?" and responded by counting the seeds in her hand. She even continued watching the seeds' development in the following weeks. This was a real breakthrough for us.

Rachel continued to ask us several questions each day, appearing to be ready to learn but as the Easter holidays drew to a close her words became more muddled than usual, climaxing in terrible moods, tantrums and her peculiar stupid behaviour for the last couple of days of the holiday. I can only assume that this was due to her anxiety about the impending new term. The first two days back at school she seemed to be tense and irritable but she told us that she had achieved a much better standard of work. She said she had managed to complete the assigned three pieces of work rather than the usual one, and had written seven lines of writing instead of the usual three lines. I couldn't wait to see her teacher to see if this was true. As she was now back at school we stopped her activity programme as planned, as we didn't want to overtire her or clash with her school work but we encouraged constructive play in a casual way whenever possible, to reinforce our holiday projects.

The next major problem for Rachel was starting Brownies. She had always wanted to join and often spoke of Brownies and "blue" Brownies as she called the Guides; Gary was a keen Cub, collecting badges down his arm and she couldn't wait to do her equivalent. We guessed that this could be difficult for her but as she was so keen we decided to give it a try. After all, Rachel had a lot of energy to use up, she was a determined little madam and we'd found a way of coping through dancing. We therefore put her name on the waiting list of a pack whose Brown Owl was a personal friend of the family and had known Rachel since she was a baby.

I thought it best not to anticipate the event too early, knowing what a state she could get into but the evening before, she remembered it herself and consequently became upset. All night she was dreaming, crying and worrying about the unknown. I think she was aware of her own limitations and was afraid she wouldn't be able to do something when asked, but in spite of all her fears she still wanted to go! Perverse creature that she was, she was determined to be a Brownie but confused and scared of yet another unknown situation. The next day was terrible but we somehow got through it, but not without Rachel achieving a temperature of a hundred and one degrees Fahrenheit. By the evening she was complaining of having a headache and earache but somehow I didn't think Rachel was really ill as she was always robust and healthy, in spite of her ridiculously diminished appetite. At the eleventh hour she started to say that she didn't want to go to Brownies that night but would start the following week! No way did I feel the family could cope with this performance twice. I'm afraid it was a case of now or never – so I decided in all our best interests to force her. I felt torn inside by doing something which deep down I felt was probably best for her, but also cruel as she cried and clung to me all the way there. I pushed her along the street on my bicycle as she couldn't walk and prayed that Viv, our friend the Brown Owl, would understand my philosophy. It seemed the Gods were against me though, as Viv was late that night and her assistant, a stranger to Rachel, was starting the meeting. I thought it best to see this thing through as we'd come so far already, so made a snap decision to sit down to watch and wait until Brown Owl arrived. When she finally came I gave her a rundown on the situation, promised to go straight home and sit by the phone in case she needed help, told Rachel that she was to try this week but need never go again if she didn't like it and then proceeded to peel her off me to make a quick getaway!

On arriving home I felt both sick and exhausted. The scene had been more like a reluctant child being dragged into the classroom on her first day at school rather than a child starting what was meant to be a voluntary club designed for youngsters to enjoy! A quarter of an hour before Brownies ended I was there, ready to meet her, expecting a limp, exhausted child to emerge with a tear-stained face. Instead she strolled out beaming from ear to ear saying, "I want to go again, Mummy".

With the security and support of a known friend she managed to enjoy Brownies but we did have a few hiccups later on when Viv gave up being Brown Owl and Rachel had to adjust to a different leader. Badges were also a problem as again, Rachel set herself high targets of achievement. She wasn't content simply to plod through the weekly meetings, she had to have as many badges, if not more, than the best of them. This made it difficult as we had to choose all hers carefully so that she could present most of her work as already being done on the day of the test. We also tried to label everything possible so that she wasn't caught out with awkward questions. Fortunately most of the examiners were so impressed by all the extra work this involved that they rarely failed her. In this way Rachel not only got through Brownies but went on eventually to obtain her Baden Powell award, the highest badge awarded to Guides.

The following day after starting Brownies, Rachel did seem unwell so I kept her home to make sure and took her to the doctor's in the evening for a check-up. He said there was nothing wrong so I assumed it was just a reaction to all the emotion the day before. Unfortunately, Rachel had enjoyed her day off so much that she didn't want to return to school the next day, so I had to drag her there, sobbing all the way. I handed her over to her teacher who was quite sympathetic and made Rachel her special helper for the day. Whilst there I made an appointment to see her teacher the following week to see how things were progressing after all our project work.

Phil went with me that evening and we were pleased to see that her work had improved a hundred per cent. She was now consistently writing about half a page with only occasional reversals of letters, although her numbers were still often reversed. I felt particularly pleased with this as I'd done a lot of work with Rachel on letters in the holiday. I'd discovered that Rachel didn't respond to being shown or told how to produce letters but quickly learnt by tactile (touch) methods. Therefore, we wrote letters all over the place by using her finger in sand, on the carpet or embossed wallpaper and played guessing games when 'writing' on each other's backs. When I felt she'd conquered this we did a lot of rainbow writing, which involved tracing over a letter in as many different colours as possible.

The fact that her letters were now correct and we'd worked solely on letters and not numbers seemed to me that our project had been successful, so I planned to work on numbers in the same way in the summer holiday. Her pictures had also improved and she'd made a good effort at a piano, an owl and a castle. She'd also made three cards with the pictures on the front instead of her usual style of having the pictures on the back.

Altogether she was a different child; more relaxed, happy and confident, which was no doubt helped by the fact that she could now ride her bicycle as well. This change in Rachel was noticed and remarked upon by several different people.

Chapter Five
Projects and Problems

During the next half-term holiday, which was Whitsun, I decided to do something to try to improve Rachel's concepts and logical thinking, so I borrowed some big wooden association plaques from the hearing impaired unit for this purpose. Rachel was keen to play with them but really had no idea how to use them. They felt good to hold and were attractively painted, being designed rather like dominoes with two pictures of simple objects on each plaque. The idea was not to match them but to put together two pictures with some association to each other – it could be two pieces of furniture, two things of the same colour, both having wheels or the same background colour. It could be played as simply or as cleverly as the players wished but my idea was to stretch her vocabulary and to get her thinking logically about explaining things. At first the game was little more than hard work; she knew she had to look for clues but failed to see even the obvious. Not only that, I was horrified to discover just how limited her vocabulary was. I was shocked to realise through playing the game that although she knew words like 'bed' and 'table' she didn't know the word 'furniture'; likewise with apples and bananas, she didn't know they were both fruits. This seemed to apply to most group nouns but with other things it seemed she knew the group name like 'flowers' and 'birds' but not their individual names like 'daisy', 'bluebell', 'parrot' or 'peacock'. Fortunately she liked playing with the plaques and as I always found with her, it was amazing how quickly she improved in such situations.

Also in that holiday, we did our planned work on her reversal of numbers to see if we could achieve the same level of success as we had with the letters – although I was disappointed to see that she still did occasionally do some letter reversals and pictures on the backs of cards. At least she was nothing like as bad as she had been originally.

By surreptitiously providing the right play materials we tried to improve her confidence in tracing and colouring as well and hoped that the weather would allow us to try to get her into the water as I knew swimming would start in school during the next half of the term and so far Rachel would only tolerate water ankle deep, after which she froze and screamed with fear!

Everything seemed to go well that holiday, spending about half an hour in the morning and another half an hour later in the day on our little projects, but the weather was too cold for swimming and the petrol shortage of 1979 prevented us from going to the nearest indoor pool.

On returning to school I was delighted to see that all our holiday work had paid off again. Her language was still muddled at times but the temper tantrums seemed to be lessening and she appeared to become more confident and less dependent on me. Her school work was also improving including her drawings and writing of numbers and she would now initiate a discussion or conversation. Another improvement was the way in which she played. For one thing she was beginning to play with normal children nearer her own age rather than younger or slow-learning children; she played alone for the first time and was now able to play games which involved rules rather than just acting out a mothers and babies-type game.

The next hurdle in Rachel's life was that Gary began to enjoy having piano lessons and Rachel couldn't see why she wasn't allowed to have a try too. We weren't at all sure that she was ready for such lessons but every day when Gary practised she insisted on trying to copy him until in the end we discussed the situation with the piano teacher rather hoping that she would make the negative decision for us. Instead she said that as Rachel had a good reading age at school, in spite of everything else, she was willing to try teaching her, so of course Rachel was delighted with the verdict. We agreed to go along with it as long as everyone was happy. After all, I supposed it would reinforce her left and right concepts and help to broaden her horizons if nothing else, but I wondered how on earth her teacher would cope, because I didn't think Rachel could discriminate between notes going up and down visually let alone aurally in music.

In June we finally got Rachel willingly to enter the sea, albeit she only went knee-deep. Although I was pleased I was still aware that she'd have to go in deeper water for swimming at school but fortunately that hadn't started yet. As Rachel was no better in the public swimming pool, preferring to stay in the paddling pool and screaming if we took her into the shallow end of the big pool, we chose to save our money and stay on the beach. At least she would play on the sand now! One good thing to come out of these trips was that at last she managed to catch a large beach ball when it was thrown to her at close range! Eventually, after many trips and inexhaustible patience (which I must admit came close to being exhausted at times!) we managed to get her into the water waist-deep but she wrapped her body around mine and clung on like grim death! She didn't like it but she tolerated it, so I felt that was enough; I'd leave the rest for the school to cope with. We did manage to play a splashing game which she enjoyed when knee-deep but again she clung very firmly on to my hand. I noticed that when walking out of the water she would *not* walk through any seaweed and for some reason or other she seemed to be convinced that all the boats would overturn and all the people would drown! Was there no end to this girl's fears?

Well, the day for swimming lessons at school arrived and although she went off happily enough that day, the previous evening had been terrible! Her language had been very mixed up and she was unable to ask me if Daddy had mended the puncture in her bicycle tyre. She ended up having a terrible tantrum, lying on the floor, hammering her heels and fists into the carpet and sobbing inconsolably. This went on for about twenty minutes before I was able to calm her down, sit down quietly with her and try to sort out exactly what she wanted to say. This was the first tantrum for ages but unfortunately it wasn't to be the last. After that we had word swapping all evening and she was unable to do her evening reading from her school book although she tried as usual when Gary did his. She read lots of words reversed like "on" for "no", swapped around the order of the words in the sentence and even read the lines in the wrong order.

Her language continued to be her main problem and we had many similar episodes of frustration leading to temper tantrums which lasted anything up to half an hour when she couldn't explain things or ask us something which was important to her. Even a simple statement like, "Dancing is at six o'clock," proved too difficult for her one day so we had all the usual heart-rending sobbing and thrashing about until she said, "Dancing is in half a – um – um – clock – you know – on the six." Her frustration always continued until we'd established *exactly* what she meant.

Sometimes she wasn't really aware of her errors as long as we knew what she meant. One day she came up to me with both hands behind her back and instead of asking me, "In which hand is the brown crayon?" she asked "What colour is brown?" Luckily I responded and guessed correctly so the incident passed unnoticed by Rachel.

Another problem that occurred due to her lack of understanding was when her grandparents went on holiday to Ireland. Rachel knew they were going on a boat so, as usual, she had little faith in their ability to stay afloat! She seemed convinced that even if the boat succeeded in miraculously getting them there, they wouldn't be able to return even if they chose to do so. I don't know to what pagan establishment she felt they were going but it all seemed to be beyond her comprehension. I spent hours with her using a globe, drawing pictures and crossing off days on a special calendar until they returned, bringing many small gifts for her and her brother. I think she had some understanding of the situation in the end but it had certainly been a stressful time for her.

Although Rachel still used word substitutes and muddled words like "undo" and "do up", it was obvious to us that she was trying hard to understand things now. I think this was what led to the increase in her frustration tantrums. We noticed that she would query what a new word meant when she heard or saw one she didn't remember but she never used it herself afterwards. Her reading age was very good in spite of occasionally reversing words, changing the word order or missing out lines! However, if we asked her a question about what she had just read she could rarely explain the story or meaning of the text. I think she did what was generally referred to as 'barking at print'. All in all though, in spite of her teacher reporting that she needed a lot of individual attention, we could see that some progress had been made in all areas that term for which we felt extremely grateful.

Her main problem continued to be her poor use of vocabulary and her inability to understand any intellectual conversation no matter how it was presented to her. She was the complete opposite of Gary who soaked up information like a sponge, but with the experience I'd gained from teaching the deaf children I felt I should have been able to get through to her better than I did. She would hold a gentle conversation with us, ask some questions and even answer simple questions in a one-to-one situation but otherwise she appeared to let things go completely over her head unless she was directly involved.

By the end of June, Rachel was becoming a much more affectionate child. I can well remember one afternoon when she saw my mother walking up the road as she arrived for a visit; Rachel spontaneously ran up to her and gave her a hug which surprised my mother into saying "She's quite nice now, isn't she?" Now my mother is a very dutiful person who loved all her grandchildren equally and although I'm sure she could have bitten off her tongue when she realised what she'd said, I knew exactly what she meant!

Rachel was becoming happier and more confident; although her fears were still there, they were definitely diminishing. Also, she was beginning to cope with and enjoy playing games like snap or snakes and ladders with us now but thank goodness she didn't seem to need the constant company any more.

Eventually we were told that Kevin Brown would be able to see Rachel in school on July 5th 1979, after which he would do a home visit to discuss the results with us. In spite of all Rachel's progress I couldn't wait to hear his opinion of her.

Chapter Six

Let Battle Commence

It was Rachel's open evening on July 4th 1979, the day before Kevin would do his educational psychological assessment of her in school. All day at work I was feeling apprehensive about how the school staff would react towards us regarding the impending investigation, knowing that we had instigated it ourselves. So far there had been no reaction from them whilst waiting for it to arrive so I hoped they would continue in the same vein. Instinctively though, I expected to face some reaction that evening. Julie reassured me during our lunch-time chat that they could do absolutely nothing to stop the investigation and told me that if any comments were made against it we could reply that we knew our parental rights and that was what we wanted. On arriving home from work we both washed and changed to present ourselves in our best light, in spite of the fact that they had seen one or both of us twice a day ever since she had started at the school! At least it improved my confidence. On the way there I told Phil what Julie had said but it seemed he wasn't as bothered about their opinions as I was and already felt that way. He did admit that it was nice to know that we would be correct in saying such a thing in defence of our actions should it prove necessary though.

On examination of her work all our opinions about her improvement were confirmed. Her reading age was high, her written work was much better with only occasional reversals of letters now and she had achieved a good standard in maths. Her pictures were much improved generally in as much as the people had gained more detail as she seemed to be adding things like arms and hands but she still only concentrated on drawing houses, trees and flowers whenever possible. Her teacher was a kindly Scottish lady who did her best to support Rachel in class and told us not to worry about her because she felt Rachel just lacked confidence and simply needed lots of reassurance. Well, I'd spent the last seven years telling Rachel that being nice was much more important than being clever but so far it'd had little effect! We said nothing to this comment but were surprised when she went on to say that the Headmistress had asked to see us before we went home. We therefore proceeded immediately to the Head's inner sanctum, feeling somewhat like lambs going to the slaughter but with Phil reminding me all the time that there was nothing to get worried about. They couldn't stop us and it may even be about something else other than the assessment.

However, it seemed all my feelings of apprehension had been justified and I was more than grateful for Julie's advice and support. Her phrase about "knowing our parental rights" kept floating about in my head whilst the Head sat there telling us that she felt Rachel just needed more confidence. We politely listened but I was shocked to hear her say that she felt Rachel could be inhibited by our expectations! We tried to discuss things with the Head, saying that we knew Rachel was a nervous child but denied asking too much from her. We had always told her that she could only do her best and not to worry about the standard achieved, as we would help her overcome anything that worried her should her teachers want more. I explained that Rachel had always been in awe of her brother and could be inhibited by his achievements, as she used to be upset when he could read but she couldn't, but that didn't apply now. Rachel herself was a perfectionist who set herself high standards. If Rachel wanted to show us something like a handstand, we would watch and dutifully admire the demonstration but if she knew she could do better, she would not accept our congratulations but would insist on trying again until a satisfactory standard was achieved. We tried to explain all this to the Head and I said that I would send in my diaries on Rachel for her to read but it was obvious that she had already formed her opinion and was only intent on persuading us to cancel the next day's appointment. We politely quoted our prepared phrase. I remember saying to her that should we be proven wrong after the assessment that I would apologise to her but should we be proven right I would expect an apology from her. I don't think she answered.

On the way home I started doubting myself again and wished I could have been blessed with Phil's quiet confidence in his own opinions. How could all those professional people not see Rachel as we did? Surely they couldn't all be wrong. Admittedly she was a 'highly-strung' child to say the least; maybe they were right after all. Even so, if it was all caused by a simple lack of confidence I wanted to know why. *Why* was she *so* nervous of the unknown? I didn't believe in the Head's theory that we inhibited her, but instinctively knew that it had something to do with Rachel's understanding. I felt sure that she had some problem in comprehending language because once we managed to make her understand something, the problems surrounding that situation seemed to gradually dissolve. I was so glad that Kevin would be seeing her the next day and hoped it wouldn't be too long before he made his appointment to come and discuss it all with us.

The next day I sent my diary into school with Rachel as promised, albeit some badly written, probably emotional notes in a scrappy old notebook discarded by one of the children. I didn't care, as I felt the end justified the means. However, I was amazed at the letter I received with its return that afternoon. I don't know why but I have always kept that letter in which the Headmistress simply said:

Thank you for the notebook – herewith returned.

She went on to explain that she had chosen to see Rachel that morning to explain that Mr Brown would be seeing some children that afternoon and she had been chosen as one of them.

Didn't she trust me to explain such things to my child?

She went on to say that she had given Rachel a preliminary test which I felt was totally unfair to her. She also said that during a chat, Rachel had been able to explain about her grandparents' holiday in Ireland and their present to her of a charm for her bracelet. According to the Headmistress, Rachel had understood what was expected of her and had replied quickly throughout the test.

I felt very indignant about the whole episode. Not only was the Head subjecting Rachel to such a session knowing she was to undergo intense testing later in the day but she could have no comprehension of the abnormal amount of teaching Rachel had needed in order to understand about her grandparents' holiday. Not only that, Rachel had obviously forgotten about all the other little presents she had received apart from the charm! By the time I had read the last paragraph I was completely incensed. In this she had concluded that Rachel did not produce the symptoms of stress that we observed because she was relaxed and at ease in school. She suggested that we could be unconsciously expecting Rachel to get muddled – so she did – much as if one visits an austere aunt who you know expects you to drop one of her best glasses – so you do!

She finished by informing me that Rachel had been seen by Mr Brown who would be in touch with us.

I couldn't believe that I had received such a letter from a professional person and thanked God that Kevin had assessed her that day. Although Phil was equally as furious at the tone of the letter he felt that as we had got the assessment we wanted, it would now be best to wait quietly for the result. We had caused enough ripples so did not want to cause any more. Quite honestly I don't think either of us could have written a reply to that letter. It didn't seem to deserve one.

Although it seemed like an eternity Kevin did actually arrange to come and see us on the evening of July 11th 1979. I cannot explain the feeling of relief I felt whilst talking to him, as it became apparent that he not only understood everything we were trying to say but also agreed with us that Rachel did in fact have very severe specific learning difficulties. He also said that she was behaving as he'd expect for a child born as she was in such a hurry. He wasn't surprised that she saw fear in everything and told us that with her anxiety and degree of problems he was surprised that she was not worse than she was! He even congratulated us on our handling of her; he was the first professional to acknowledge our problems and not criticise our methods of coping with them. He also said that he could see Rachel had also suffered from poor motor control (co-ordination and muscle control) and spatial problems (awareness of position and how everything relates to something next to it – important for reading and writing) but thanks to our help and her IQ, which was about a hundred and twenty, she had achieved a reasonable standard for a seven year old. It seemed that she had actually scored an eight to eight-and-a-half year level in some tests but had failed four of the five sections tested. Her problems included poor motor control, spatial problems and crossed laterality (a right-handed person should develop right-sided dominance but Rachel used either hand, foot and eye, which meant her brain hadn't developed a dominant side). She had problems sequencing a series of items such as pictures, numbers, letters or instructions and she had trouble in interpreting information even when it was presented visually. Kevin remarked upon Rachel's extreme tension and determination to succeed at the highest possible level and said that without that determination her scores would have been a lot lower with her degree of problems. It was seeing that amount of effort which was needed all the time in order for her to keep up, even at a low level, that broke my heart and I was glad that he had acknowledged it.

Kevin finished his visit by offering to see Rachel on a weekly basis to help relieve some of the tension present, to try to improve her confidence and find out about any other underlying cause for all her fears. At the same time he would guide us through a remedial programme of academic activities and recommended some suitable play materials obtainable at the toy library and some workbooks that would be useful for us to use at home. I did ask Kevin about my theory that Rachel might have an underlying language problem but he said he wasn't sure, but as she had such gross learning difficulties, he recommended getting rid of them first and then seeing what we were left with. I vaguely recalled Julie saying that if Rachel had got a language disorder, she thought that Kevin would notice it, so, at the time, this seemed reasonably sensible and we were glad to accept the advice and support from the first person to offer any real help apart from Julie.

We soon fell into a routine of weekly sessions after school with Kevin, which Rachel enjoyed immensely. She idolised him and worked hard at everything he suggested, after which he would have a chat with either Phil or me to see how Rachel had coped that week when we went to collect her. In this way he supported us all as a family and guided us through the recommended workbooks and activities at home. In order to accommodate this half hour every day it proved necessary to fit it in as soon as seemed reasonable after her drink and biscuits on arriving home from school while she was still geared up to work. Unfortunately this meant that Phil often came home from work to find me sitting down at the table working away with Rachel or quietly trying to explain something to her. On these days he was quite happy to set to and cook the evening meal; in fact he said he preferred the role of chef to being Rachel's tutor, so fortunately we all slotted nicely into our niches.

To wait until after the evening meal would have been impossible because of all the children's activities such as Cubs, Brownies, dancing, gymnastics and performing in the local pantomime. We seriously wondered if the children should give up some of their hobbies as they were becoming harder to fit into an already tight schedule but quite honestly this was the area where Rachel was able to relax and enjoy herself away from school. Not only that, we felt a lot of her hobbies were actually helping her both remedially and by boosting her self-respect and confidence. However, it wasn't all play as Rachel would work extremely hard to keep up her quota of Brownie badges and would work morning, noon and night to learn a new dance routine once I had been to the lesson to write down the steps for her to remember. One girl who stayed with us for eighteen months and subsequently became a family friend can well remember Rachel practising her tap routines on the kitchen floor before going to school each morning. I think she found it more effective than her alarm!

Chapter Seven
Confusion, Fears and Phobias

That summer holiday we continued with half an hour a day working in her recommended workbook but otherwise just concentrated on enjoying the holiday and basically broadening her horizons. It was good to see a gradual improvement in her fine motor control, but she still couldn't write on lines, which would soon be expected of her in junior school. I was aware though that there would be plenty of others in the same boat and I knew there were much more important things to work on first.

I still felt her language was the biggest problem which in turn led to a lack of understanding, which ultimately resulted in a most amazing list of fears and phobias. I was convinced that her lack of language was the crux of the whole matter but everyone else seemed to think she was okay, just shy and not as bright as I thought she was. Although she was beginning to improve in her discussion and take an intelligent interest in some things, I couldn't help feeling concerned about the way she still muddled her words.

One day she wanted to ask if we could have shepherd's pie for dinner but just couldn't make me understand what she wanted for a long time. She ended up having another lengthy tantrum, lasting a good twenty minutes until finally, through a process of elimination, I guessed correctly what she meant. She began by saying, "Can we have um, um, um – something for dinner – you know..." She tried to explain but just got confused and more and more frustrated. "Potatoes with little bits in" was tried, so I showed her the potato salad with chives in the fridge thinking I'd got it at last. No that wasn't it – she meant meat with little bits in. Now I knew she loved salami so I took that out of the fridge to show her. Finally, after much sobbing and thrashing about until we were both exhausted, emotionally if not physically, we established that she wanted little bits of meat with potato on top! She was seven years old and still couldn't ask for a favourite meal. I don't know who hurt the most.

Another time that led to a similar episode revolved around food again. Phil had gone out, but unknown to me he had told Rachel that he would bring back some fancy cakes for tea as a treat. She was obviously delighted and wanted to pass on the information to me but she failed completely to convey this message. I thought she was asking if Daddy would bring something back but as I knew he hadn't gone to collect anything I kept explaining that, "No, he isn't bringing anything back". Understandably this distressed her very much as she was looking forward to the cakes, but I just couldn't fathom out what the problem was until Phil finally returned bearing the gift of fancy cakes for tea!

One of the biggest things she had to cope with that summer was the unexpected arrival of our Swedish penfriends which completely disrupted any plans we may have made previously. I hadn't realised before how much I had explained to Rachel about any family plans for such things as excursions, which of course we always followed unless prevented by an emergency or some such event. Now here we were suddenly following another family's plans which seemed to be constantly changing. Our week was turned upside down and although everyone else enjoyed it, Rachel seemed to find it very hard to cope with. I couldn't prepare her adequately for anything in advance because even when I explained the plan to her so that she understood, we often changed our programme due to the weather or because we had run out of time. Consequently she felt insecure, confused and frustrated. We seemed to spend a lot of time on the beach with our guests and although Rachel now tolerated the sand and sea, she would *not* go near any seaweed; neither would she walk on the pier because it was made of planks of wood which didn't quite meet, which meant we could see glimpses of the sea beneath. She was so frightened by this that she cried and clung on to us even when carried over it – and her fear of boats seemed to be becoming an obsession rather like her fear of motorbikes.

Later that month when Gary went to Cub camp for a week she felt worried and insecure all the time he was away. Even when we went to visit his camp site she 'froze' at the entrance and had to be carried in. Yet again, she was afraid of another unknown situation. After seeing that it was a reasonably normal, safe place she relaxed and enjoyed the visit. I was beginning to realise that we could never really prepare Rachel for anything by giving her explanations because she only really understood by actually experiencing it herself.

Whilst still in the area we thought we'd visit a large tank museum, which Phil was interested in seeing. Again Rachel didn't want to go as she couldn't absorb the information we were trying to give her. She knew that tanks were big and that soldiers had used them for fighting in the past but she was definitely afraid to go and see them. Apparently she thought they might move or maybe even start firing and no amount of reassurance would convince her that they were secured and not being operated in that setting. Again we had to carry her into the museum but initially she refused to explore the tanks with the other children. Gradually she realised that everything seemed to be safe and that nothing untoward had happened when the children climbed over the tanks, until eventually she plucked up enough courage to sit in a tank herself. By the end of the day we were even able to explain to her a little about their use in the war and she showed an intelligent curiosity. It was wonderful to see her being interested and responsive. At times I felt we were being cruel to Rachel when we pushed her into situations but I always came out feeling we had done the right thing by overcoming another obstacle. I was afraid that if we let her fears govern her life, she would not only miss out on a lot of fun but also grow into a nervous wreck! I was convinced that if only I could teach her that most things were under control, she would have more confidence in the world. It was just a matter of finding the right key to unlock her mind and help her understand.

As said previously, she would not go anywhere with close friends or even family unless either Phil, Gary or I were with her. Even so there were still occasions when she became upset, like the day we visited a local zoo and she flatly refused to go through a dimly lit tunnel. She reacted by doing her usual trick of freezing to the spot, holding herself ramrod stiff and making it very difficult to carry her – although by now I think Phil was becoming quite an expert carrier!
Another day a family friend took Gary and her bowling and although she appeared to cope with this quite well, her behaviour was diabolical in the evening after they returned home. She was swearing, shouting, angry, moody and upset about anything and everything but we could not understand why. We simply put her to bed and hoped for peace in the morning.

Because Rachel saw danger in so many things she remained overprotective of her younger cousin Brett, and her eating habits still remained another problem, although they were inclined to be inconsistent. I therefore thought that this was most likely to be manipulative behaviour being used for effect, rather like her 'hypochondria'. She either had a very low pain threshold or she was using more attention-seeking tactics.

Rachel was also genuinely worried about her brother's health because he often had large lumps and bumps on his head, especially his forehead, and had even suffered concussion two or three times because of bruising of the brain due to his undiagnosed haemophilia. This often scared Rachel. One day when he had a bad cut on the back of his head at school she confided in me that she was afraid he might die because he had lost a lot of blood. In actual fact the whole incident had been far more dramatic than serious.

Although she enjoyed visiting the theatre she always had mixed feelings about the cinema because we nearly always entered into a darkened room. She often found the climax of the film, both at the cinema and at home on television, upsetting, so subsequently she rarely watched TV and had to be assured that any visit to the cinema would not be traumatic before agreeing to accompany us on a trip.

Another problem with Rachel, due to her lack of language, was her poor memory. We had often taken the children on isolated day trips to London for different reasons, which Gary always enjoyed, absorbing all the history and atmosphere, but unless we had living proof to prompt her memory, Rachel always seemed to forget about it soon afterwards. It was very frustrating. Because Rachel was adamant that she had never been to London and seemed to have no comprehension of its importance to England, we decided to dedicate a week to day trips – 'doing the sights' and making sure that she had her photograph taken at as many famous places as seemed reasonable. We chose to use slides so that we could make a bigger impact when showing them to her at regular intervals afterwards and went to a lot of trouble preparing her for the trips, to make sure she would understand as much as possible by using lots of simple but well-illustrated children's guide books. Consequently Buckingham Palace, the coronation chair and coach and 10 Downing Street all meant something to her for the first time and we were rewarded by her questions and interest on the trip. However, I don't think we entirely succeeded because when we arrived at Buckingham Palace Rachel was convinced that the Queen would be sure to invite us in for cup of tea should she see us there! It seemed she was not to be deterred either when this failed to happen, as Rachel only became even more adamant when we went to 10 Downing Street that the Prime Minister would definitely ask us inside for some refreshment.

We spent several weeks talking about our proposed excursions which would include three or four trips to London, planning what each day should cover. Phil and I thought that we should include a ride on the underground one day during the trips and we also thought we'd try to conquer her fear of boats, once and for all, by incorporating a river trip from Westminster to Greenwich on another day. Once Rachel knew of these two excursions she began to become very, very difficult to live with. We needed to exercise an incredible amount of patience for as much as one or two weeks (on and off) prior to a visit, especially the last two days preceding the anticipated event. Even so she became impossible and 'froze' nearer the actual time. Unfortunately, any less preparation could lead to real hysteria and even bigger problems. The day before the river trip Rachel was tense and irritable, probably because of her fear of boats, and she stayed close beside me all the time. I just gritted my teeth and tried to carry on as normally as possible – but it wasn't easy. Fortunately, our tactics paid off as she successfully 'suffered' the journey up the river, after which we all had a pleasant day. The tube also needed the same routine of reassurance with her being carried on board, but passed by quickly without too much trauma being involved.

Her final fear that summer holiday was concerned with her transfer to junior school. She was quite familiar with the actual building, staff and numbers of children because Gary was already attending but we were now having tears about writing stories. She was obviously very worried about this and I knew it would be impossible for her to write more than about two or three lines. I presumed we would just have to cope with each step at a time and hoped she would have a sympathetic teacher or that Kevin Brown would be able to help her.

Rachel at four months.

Rachel at six months with her parents and brother Gary.

Rachel leapt onto her playgroup leader's lap for security when Father Christmas arrived at their party. He was just one of her many phobias.

Rachel enjoyed dancing, which was a fun way to reinforce left and right sequencing.

Brownie Rachel with her brother Gary in cub uniform. Starting Brownies was a major problem for Rachel as she was scared of unknown situations.

Rachel on a trip to London being encouraged by her mother to stroke the Life Guard's horse.

Rachel with her Guide Captain and Commisioner after receiving her
Baden Powell award.

Rachel (back row, fifth from left) with fellow NNEB students at
college.

Chapter Eight
Is Help on the Way?

In spite of all her apprehension, Rachel seemed to sail into junior school without any problems at all. This may have been an improvement on her part or could have been due to her familiarity with the campus, which must have paid untold dividends; she was also fortunate enough to have Gary's previous class teacher whom she knew, plus the unexpected transfer of one of her infant teachers to the junior staff, which made another familiar face to whom she could refer. I know that Gary's presence in the school was her biggest support though, which was proven one day when he stayed home with yet another ear infection and Rachel refused to go to school without him. Although she went under protest it was obvious that she felt insecure knowing he wouldn't be around all day even though they would have been in different classrooms.

As the term progressed her moods began to change as Gary was doing well with lots of team points as merit awards and had become a free reader. I'm afraid she felt very inferior as all her efforts, which were always immense, were apparently going by unacknowledged. She began to say that she didn't like school because she was afraid of being told off and one day I had to collect her at lunchtime because she claimed to feel unwell. However, she seemed perfectly all right once she arrived home! Altogether we were quite pleased with the way she had coped with the major change from infants to juniors and her general improvement, plus the fact that she was beginning to be able to reveal her thoughts to us.

At open evening we were pleased to learn that Rachel was able to start on the junior school reading scheme and her handwriting was much improved although still not on the line, but as usual, she wanted to run before she could walk and was upset because everyone else was doing "joined-up" writing! Her main problem now was coping with tens and units, which we resolved to work on in the next holiday. Although we had all liked her teacher in the past and thought we'd established a good rapport, I'm afraid this was no longer the case now that she had Rachel instead of Gary to teach. In fact she told us in no uncertain terms that it was a pity we had ever seen Kevin Brown and told us that we were pushing Rachel to try to achieve what was beyond her capabilities. I tried to explain that in fact we were doing just the opposite as, apart from using Kevin Brown's books, all our activities had revolved around taking her back to reception infant work, in order to establish basic patterning for writing letters and numbers. I explained to her why we felt that this had been successful as it had always been followed by an improvement in the specific area on which we'd worked, but she dismissed that by saying it must have been pure coincidence each time. When I asked what she would have done to help her child that she was dragging to school daily, sobbing because she couldn't cope, she didn't answer – but I later found out that she was in fact pregnant with her first child. I couldn't help wondering how much she could actually relate to our situation but I knew for certain that she didn't approve of us helping Rachel or involving Kevin Brown.

That autumn Rachel 'bravadoed' herself into attending a Hallowe'en party and was even more pleased with herself when she won first prize as a witch. She was also more at ease at the bonfire parties that year, allowing herself to wander away from us a little at times.

Unfortunately, this new-found confidence and self respect was soon to take a great knock when the game of jacks became the latest craze. Rachel had already said she wanted some for Christmas and we had decided to leave it till then knowing how difficult it would be for her to cope with. The game consists of throwing a very small ball into the air and catching it with one hand whilst at the same time, picking up one or more of the five small metal objects called jacks. As Rachel still had trouble catching a larger ball with two hands she would not find it easy to cope with everything that jacks entailed.

For a couple of days Rachel became very difficult and hard to live with but finally revealed that no one would let her play jacks with them at school because she was "silly and stupid at it". She was particularly hurt when her best friend also refused to let her join in the game. The next morning it all came to a head when she sobbed and messed about instead of getting herself ready for school. Her behaviour became quite out of hand as she resorted to the 'loopy' and ridiculous 'highly-strung' behaviour that she had used when younger to avoid conversations. I really didn't know what to do to pacify her so let her carry on and just tried to contain the situation, until she finally calmed down – shattered but still upset. In order to get her to school in a happy frame of mind I promised to buy her some jacks the same day. That evening she only took about two steps inside the front door when she sat down on the floor with her coat still on to open the packet and tried to play the game. Of course she couldn't even catch the ball with two hands let alone one! Obviously this led to more inevitable frustration, followed by a lot of temper at times and occasional bursts of tears but fortunately we had no tantrums.

It nearly broke my heart, knowing how hurt she was, whilst being totally unable to help her. All I could do was watch her desperate attempts to catch that wretched ball and let her work it through for herself. I think it was one of the hardest things I'd ever had to do.

She hardly moved from that spot all evening, trying all the time to learn to catch that elusive ball. The next morning she practised again before school and again in the evening, using every spare minute between coming home from school and bedtime. She really pushed herself and nothing else was allowed to take precedence. It took all my strength to help her cope but I found it very hard indeed to keep my temper with all her stupid and babyish behaviour which accompanied her efforts. Eventually after nearly a week of intense practice she felt competent enough to take her own jacks to school to play alongside her friends. Even though she hadn't become an accomplished player she could at least keep up with the peer group pressure of owning and appearing to play jacks.

Christmas brought its usual amount of excitement into the household which led Rachel into her usual regression of muddled words, frustration and tantrums but on the whole we all coped quite well. One day she wanted to ask me what her zodiacal birth sign was but as it came completely out of the blue I had no idea what she meant when she came up to me and asked, "What's my name?" Well, I knew she was confused but I didn't think she was that bad, but nevertheless, I told her the obvious and said, "Rachel." "No, what am I?" she asked. "A girl," I replied, getting equally as confused and frustrated by the conversation! Eventually by a process of elimination and a twenty questions-type game we were able to decode her question and established that her sign was Aries. Much to her satisfaction and our relief!

There were also some letter reversals in her writing but the bonus of the holiday was that she learnt to catch a ball properly. She even managed to catch it one handed when a ball was thrown to her from a distance of about fourteen feet (four metres) and learnt to catch balls that were bounced to her. That Christmas we gave Rachel a watch with the words half, quarter, past, to and o'clock written on it as well as the usual numbers in the hope that it would help her.

For our work on tens and units Phil made her a hundred one centimetre cubes (to represent units) and ten rods measuring ten centimetres by one centimetre (to represent tens). By laying down ten of the little cubes alongside a rod she could see that ten units were the same as one ten. These worked quite successfully and she was able to use them whenever she had any tens and units addition to do at home. She religiously counted out all the necessary cubes for the units and then swapped them over in groups of tens for the rods until she could see how many units were left to write in the answer box. Then she would count up her tens column including any she had carried over from the units, and consequently got the right answer. I don't think she entirely understood the concept for some time and she certainly needed to use the cubes and rods as a prop for a very long time but the tension was eased and she began to get more ticks in her maths book. No doubt her teacher felt it was another coincidence but we were happy that she had crossed another hurdle.

Although Rachel was making steady progress in most areas, albeit a long way behind her peers, her piano teacher told us what we had expected to hear a lot earlier. Although she had coped initially, Rachel had now reached a stage when she was making no further progress; she couldn't cope so the teacher thought it best to stop the lessons. I hated telling Rachel and felt guilty for having let her try when I saw how devastated she was. I had hoped that she would have come to the same decision herself first, but far from it. Rachel was still just as determined to be as good as her friends.

At times of despair I used to think that maybe Rachel would have been better off and happier in a different family or environment where she wouldn't have been surrounded by so many people succeeding in so many different areas, but in my heart I knew that we had to carry on supporting her and teaching her ourselves in the only way we knew how, which was basically by following our gut instincts! Even so, when Rachel said she wanted to learn the recorder if she couldn't do the piano my heart sank into my boots! I honestly didn't think she would cope, as one reason she had given up piano was because she couldn't distinguish whether the notes were going up or down on the music, and I was sure she wouldn't manage in the group situation at school.

I ignored her requests to pursue the recorder until one day she found my old descant recorder under a pile of sheet music. She then sat on the stairs and proceeded to expose us to all the usual horrible squeaks and squeals that most parents of recorder enthusiasts have experienced at one time or another. There was nothing for it but to appease her by trying to get a proper note out of the thing. It took me ages to succeed, after which she wanted to learn more. I showed her a simple scale of three notes using three fingers and hoped this would satisfy her until she became bored but she just kept on pestering me to let her join the recorder club. I really felt she wouldn't cope with another failure so soon and I knew that I wasn't ready for it at all!

Kevin Brown agreed with us that the recorder club would be too difficult for her, but Rachel would not accept it. Then I had a brainwave and went to see a neighbour who lived a few doors along our road. Her husband was a Baptist minister who was also an organ enthusiast, having made a few records. The whole family, including the three daughters, was very musical, and this kind, gentle lady also helped out at Rachel's school in the music department on frequent occasions, playing the piano at school concerts and, I'd discovered, by running the recorder clubs. I decided to explain everything to her and to ask if she thought she could help Rachel by perhaps giving her some private lessons at home, at her own pace and in a simplified way, until she was either able to join a suitable group at school or was bored enough to give up herself. To my immense relief and gratitude she agreed to help, so Rachel began private recorder lessons, weekly after school, which proved amazingly successful. This lovely lady managed to find a super music book, which used an extremely simple layout with large notes printed on the lines. Each page moved the pupil on in easy stages and must have been designed for young infants, but Rachel didn't care as she was happy to be learning music again. This scheme proved so successful that Rachel eventually merged with a group run by the same teacher at school.

The first year in junior school continued more or less uneventfully with only a few minor hiccups, like the time the Headmaster phoned me to say that I was wasting my money buying school dinners for Rachel, as she was persistently taking the minimum allowed and leaving the maximum amount accepted! It was agreed that she would change to sandwiches and not be allowed to throw anything away at school, so that we could monitor her eating ourselves.

The next time I had a phone call from the school was to tell me to meet them in casualty as Rachel had broken the school rule and run in the classroom. Consequently she had slipped, hit her head on the side of a desk and cut her ear which needed three stitches. She was in such a state of shock that she coped remarkably well but when she went back for their removal the poor girl was so scared she couldn't even cry. She just sat there shaking like a leaf and whimpering like a lost puppy. She looked really pathetic but I was proud of the way she managed to behave as she was no worse for the doctor to handle than any other child would have been. It was some time later that Rachel told me that she wasn't actually running in the classroom but skipping back to her seat because she was so happy! Apparently the teacher had just given Rachel her first merit mark for effort!

Rachel also coped well with the school swimming lessons in as much as we didn't have any scenes, but we made little actual progress as she was still tense in the water. I remember she was in the walking race at the swimming gala with all the other non-swimmers as every child took part in the end-of-term display, but we were glad that she was able to enjoy the event as this was a big step forward for her in itself.

She continued to work willingly and diligently through Kevin's workbooks which were beginning to become difficult for her. The work designed to improve her motor skills and visual perception (understanding what she saw) was at just the right level but the part designed to improve her language and intellectual comprehension was too hard in places. At times we would leave that section and then go back to it some weeks later which seemed to help.

By the time she was eight years old, Rachel's language remained the hardest part to cope with. As she had no real concept of time, anything in the future was always referred to as "tomorrow" and anything in the past was automatically labelled "yesterday". However, we were now blessed with the word that most parents of toddlers dread to hear: "Why?" This had become a new but well-voiced word in her vocabulary, along with her gradual desire to learn and improve her general knowledge. As this had been such a long-awaited event we were thrilled and enjoyed the novelty of being able to explain things to her.

That summer Rachel chose to go with her Brownies on pack holiday and we were delighted as she had refused to go previously. No doubt she felt more comfortable about the idea since we had camped as a family and had also helped out at Gary's Cub camp after Phil had become a Cub leader. Now she was ready to go off on her own without us for the first time. That pack holiday was a great success as she came back much more mature and confident, appearing to be more at ease in her social relationships.

At the end of the first year in juniors I had another phone call from the Headmaster to ask us our opinion of Rachel and how we would feel about placing her in a class of twelve hand-picked slow-learning children for her second year. We welcomed the idea as we felt she not only needed more individual help but would be relieved of the pressure from peer group competition and trying to succeed beyond her capabilities. Personally, I felt intrigued that Rachel's class teacher, who'd tried to tell me earlier in the year that Rachel was no worse than many others, had actually recommended her for such a class, but I felt too relieved to pass any comment.

Rachel developed a lot with the teacher in the remedial class due to his special care and understanding. He was older than her previous teacher but had a wealth of experience to give accompanied by a lot of patience and genuine concern for each individual child's problem. Now that everything possible was being done for Rachel at last, Phil and I felt able to relax and accept the situation that she was just a slow learner who was making progress at her own speed. She would probably always be the same but I did hope she would manage to reach a reasonable level, enough to cope with everyday life, even if a little late. Rachel didn't always feel the same way though, so we constantly had to remind her that being nice was much more important than being clever.

Her school reports always said the same thing for every subject – good effort but slow and immature academically although some progress had been made. She did begin to swim with arm bands whilst with the remedial teacher, and initially she loved the class and improved by taking part in all their appropriate activities.

Towards the end of that year Rachel began to object to being in that group as other children in the school were beginning to call them names such as "baby" when they played with constructive toys. We talked to her teacher about this as it was becoming a problem. We didn't want anything to spoil what had been such a success as we knew both the teacher and the special class had been exactly what she'd needed. He then surprised us by disclosing that Rachel wasn't really like the rest of the children in his class. He said that most of them were of low ability and indicated that some had other social problems, apart from one who was there to catch up on schoolwork because she had missed a lot of schooling due to ill health, but he felt Rachel didn't really fit into any of those categories. He said she came across as a bright child and quite understood her feelings about the group and other children's teasing. He went on to say that he felt that Rachel had made sufficient progress to integrate into a normal class for three topic lessons a week which he would try to arrange for the next term. This worked extremely well as it gave a balance to Rachel's life in school. She had the support of the special class and teacher without the status of wholly belonging to the group. At the same time she could enjoy the prestige of integration without suffering the continual pressure to succeed alongside her peers.

Unfortunately she was placed in normal classes for the third and fourth years, with no extra support, but she struggled on at her own pace with no major setbacks. When she was nine years old Kevin Brown felt he had reached the end of his therapy but promised to assess her prior to her move into senior school. By now Rachel was making steady progress in all areas both at school and socially at Brownies and dancing. At the end of her fourth year in juniors her class teacher made an interesting observation when the class were doing a special test. It was during a multiple choice Richmond test paper, when he noticed that Rachel was what he described as a "belt and braces" type of person who needed the double security of checking everything twice over. He went on to describe how he had watched her repeatedly rereading all the questions and answers before attempting to answer them, so much so that she only completed a quarter of the paper in the allotted time – but had actually answered every question attempted correctly. Although she'd scored a hundred per cent in her work her mark was recorded as being twenty-five per cent because of the amount achieved. Her teacher said he suspected Rachel had slow thought processes, which proved to be a very accurate statement if only we'd known why at the time.

Chapter Nine
Still More Struggles

When Rachel was eleven years old her brother spent a few months in a London hospital which, of course, involved a lot of family visiting. He was in a large children's ward which had an excellent play leader who inspired Rachel into realising that this was an area of work in which she would like to be trained. She had always had a natural ability to work well with children and had enjoyed the challenge of helping with the deaf children in my unit at work but now, I think she fully realised for the first time that she would like to work with handicapped or sick children in some way.

She continued to develop socially and grow in confidence but still needed a lot of our support at times, in order to succeed. This was particularly apparent when she went on Guide camps as her Guide Captain reported to us that she had overheard Rachel talking to herself one day while she was shut in a tent alone, unaware of anyone outside who might hear her. She was heard to say repeatedly that she *was* going to stay at camp and that she *was* going to cope with everything! I don't think her leader had been fully aware of Rachel's inner struggle until that moment but something similar was noticed on each subsequent camp, even though she chose to go along each time herself! One of the things Rachel found hard at Guides, besides all the badge work, was being a patrol leader, as she lacked the authority to lead or direct girls so near to her own age, and had difficulty in coping with all their various teenage moods. Rachel found this particularly frustrating as she was so good when dealing with younger children.

Dancing continued to be of great remedial benefit to Rachel as well as a pleasure but again she continued to need extra lessons and support in learning the routines until she was nearly fifteen years old. It wasn't until then that she coped for the first time with learning five new routines in ballet, tap and modern for a show, alongside her peers in normal lessons. However, although ballet was her favourite subject she hated the improvisation that was part of that class as it required her to use imagination which she found difficult.

It was about that time that Rachel began looking for a part-time holiday job. Although she was good with children she found straightforward nannying boring, so thought she'd try for a shop assistant post, but after one morning in a busy craft shop, she was told she was too slow mentally for such work. Some time later she did manage to cope with a job in a small newsagent in one of the back streets of town, where the pace was probably slower.

It was in school where all her biggest problems seemed to lie. Although Kevin Brown had assessed her and said he thought she would cope with senior school, he then left the district and was replaced by a woman who was all but unavailable. Rachel did in fact cope initially but only just, and only by enormous efforts on her part, because it was against her nature to let herself fail if she could prevent it. Although her reading and writing skills were now of a good standard she still had occasional wrong spellings and her sentence structure was often muddled or immature. The half-hour homework per subject every night was taking her at least two hours to complete due to her 'slow thought processes', difficulty in understanding the task or text involved and her inability to decide what to write or how to answer a question, and there was often more than one subject set. Not only that, Rachel was smuggling books out of school that shouldn't have left the premises, in order to finish off class work. Sometimes she worked solidly all weekend, even with our support and often until quite late in the evening, in order to keep up. Many times we would have to make her stop to have some relaxation before going to bed. She struggled through the first year, after which we were thankful to learn that she was withdrawn from German lessons in the second year. After much discussion we managed to persuade them to withdraw her from French lessons as well and to substitute it with extra English in the remedial unit.

In view of her success with the recorder Rachel felt inspired to enrol herself for clarinet lessons in the lunch hour, along with a couple of friends. I felt she was being a little ambitious but she enjoyed the experience until all her friends moved on to the next stage and she was left in the beginners class. Fortunately the music teacher had a dyslexic mother so proved extremely sympathetic and supportive towards

Rachel, admiring her 'never say die' attitude, but eventually Rachel gave it up as a dismal failure. After that Rachel decided to try private singing lessons which finally proved to be her best musical venture. Apparently she had a promising voice and had gathered some musical knowledge over the years. At last she had found a musical outlet which could give her some satisfaction and was to be followed up later on when she joined a local musical comedy and operatic company and even enjoyed taking small parts.

Her art work had suddenly improved out of all recognition and her teacher was pleased with her efforts, but for some reason Rachel wouldn't consider it as an exam subject.

History and geography proved hard for Rachel as there were so many extra new words involved; it was like coping with another language for her. But maths and English remained hardest of all. Maths incorporated so many different sequences of instructions that she just couldn't follow, so she just plodded on in the bottom sets which did nothing for her self esteem. Even so the teachers seemed to expect her to cope with things like negative and positive numbers and percentages, which were way beyond her comprehension. Sometimes by modifying the teaching I could achieve some success at home but it took hours of practical examples to enable her to grasp the basic concept. I didn't like seeing her have to work so hard but didn't know what else to do when she was so determined not to fail. The school were convinced that she just wasn't intelligent but Rachel was adamant that she would succeed in the end. Phil and I felt out of our depth with no one to help us, so we just continued to support Rachel through the system for as long as we could.

English, both oral and written, remained a headache for us all but she refused to allow us to talk to her teachers about her problems. They rarely listened or understood anyway! In times of crisis I resorted to writing a letter to school, unknown to Rachel, or else we had to wait until open evenings which always proved the same nothing but praise for her efforts but, "Oh dear, she can't do it, can she?" Whenever we tried to explain her problems we were simply told that she wasn't as bright as we seemed to think she was but we were not to worry as there were plenty more in the school just like her.

Poor Rachel just didn't have the comprehension to cope with all that was expected of her. She was thirteen years old when she began to understand simple jokes but even then she could not grasp the meaning of the punchline if it involved a play on words or a homonym (a word sounding the same as another but with a different meaning, such as 'bear' and 'bare').

One day we were all sitting at the breakfast table when Gary asked us the question, "What did the baby chick say when the mother hen laid an orange?" The answer was "Oh, look, what Mama laid!" (said so that it sounded like marmalade). We all laughed and thought it was a good joke but Rachel became quite angry saying, "I think that's a stupid joke. Everyone knows hens lay eggs not oranges!" The whole punchline had obviously been beyond her comprehension again. Instead of laughing, I then felt more like crying as the whole situation seemed so sad.

Although Rachel's long-term memory had improved over the years she still had difficulty in remembering dates and times, or delivering a message accurately.

We had managed to buy Rachel some simplified versions of the children's classics, which she was just beginning to enjoy reading for pleasure when she was issued with a copy of *Macbeth* to study for school! The whole situation seemed so ridiculous but we felt our hands were tied and we were obliged to go along with whatever they threw at us! We managed to obtain a simplified version of the basic story and spent hours together, going over all the homework and classwork that was smuggled home, but it just resulted in tears. In the end, at her request, we managed to find two sympathetic teachers who were willing to give her private coaching in maths, when required, and English on a weekly basis.

Eventually Rachel had to choose her topics to be studied to exam level. Maths and English were compulsory but she could choose up to six others. She chose child care, needlework, and cookery and nutrition, which we felt would help her achieve her ambition to do the NNEB course in child care. Her other subjects were typing and office practice as we thought the typing would reinforce her spelling and grammar in English, and at the school's insistence she was persuaded to do history and world studies, as they felt she had chosen a rather narrow band of subjects.

It was at this time that the new examination called GCSE was introduced and Rachel's year group were to be the guinea pigs. Although I could see that this might be an advantage to Rachel as sixty per cent of the marks in some exams were based on course work, thus relieving the pressure of the final exam, I was still worried as any allowances an educational psychologist might arrange for the final papers would not necessarily carry over into the new method of continual assessment. Once more we felt at a loss as to how to help Rachel and there didn't seem to be anyone to turn to, as Kevin had moved out of the district and I had temporarily lost touch with my old friend Julie since she had moved to another county. The careers person at school had more or less laughed in our faces when Rachel said she wanted to do the NNEB course and told her (I quote), "You don't stand a hope in hell of getting into college; you'd be better off trying for a YTS (Youth Training Scheme run by the local council) course!" She was heartbroken by this rebuff but as usual responded with her phenomenal determination to succeed at all costs.

One day when I was feeling particularly low I went into my bedroom and pulled out all my old diaries in which I'd written down any significant thoughts about Rachel in an attempt to help me have some understanding of her problems. So far I had only written in those books but had never sat down in sentimental nostalgia, as I did then, to read them from cover to cover. As I read my entries it suddenly dawned on me how many times I had written that Rachel just didn't seem to understand. I had even queried a language problem with Kevin Brown at our first meeting but as with everyone else, he had brushed it aside as being unlikely. I had at one time accepted the possibility that Rachel might be dyslexic and had joined the local support group to try to identify with their problems but had found that although dyslexics had some similar problems with sequencing letters or ideas, they could usually understand conversations and explain their thoughts orally but had difficulty with the written word. They certainly didn't have Rachel's lack of understanding or strange phobias and fears of the unknown world.

I resolved then to have a proper language assessment done on Rachel, but that was easier said than done as we met with nothing but obstacles along the way. For nearly two years we did battle with educational psychologists and speech therapists, both locally and in London but they all said they were unable to do a proper assessment as Rachel was now over eleven years old but not yet an adult. On the evidence of a few tests done locally it seemed that Rachel was predisposed to having a problem but nothing more conclusive was done.

It was quite by coincidence that I had befriended a new dinner lady called Brenda at work, who had a daughter who was severely language-impaired but wished to join Brownies. I had explained how I had coped with similar problems with Rachel who was now a Young Leader at a local Brownie pack and would be only too pleased to help her daughter. In conversation I happened to mention the diaries I had kept on Rachel, which Brenda asked to read. Whilst she had them, she took it upon herself to show them to her daughter's head teacher at the language impaired unit where she went to school. On returning them, Brenda told me what she had done and that the teacher was convinced Rachel was a classic case of a language-impaired child!

I didn't know what to think at that stage but agreed to go with Brenda to the next AFASIC meeting, which was a support group for parents with language-impaired children, when a talk was to be given by a psychologist on how to recognise language-impaired four-year-olds. I would also have a chance to meet the teacher who had read my diaries.

That evening I sat and listened like someone stunned as the psychologist proceeded to describe our daughter exactly as she had been aged four! I felt both relieved and excited to know that at last I really *knew* what her problems were, without any doubt or uncertainty, but how were we to get them acknowledged by the world in general or get the necessary help for her? It seemed that the answer was also on hand that night as Brenda's friend, the teacher, was willing to refer Rachel for a full language assessment, to a friend of hers – who just happened to be the Chief Speech Therapist at The Newcomen Centre at Guy's Hospital in London. I couldn't believe my luck that night. Maybe our struggle was nearly over!

At the end of Rachel's fourth year at senior school we reviewed all her exam subjects with her teachers. Her best subject was child care but even in that she had problems with medical terminology and basic biology related to conception, problems in pregnancy and contraception. Cookery was okay but the theory for nutrition was another new language for her which needed a great deal of work on the different food values. I ended up making her a simple picture book to give her a visual image of the different categories and their functions. Needlework was fine and typing was adequate but slow. For this we bought her a typewriter for Christmas so that she could keep plodding away at home in order to help her keep up. Maths and

English were in hand with the extra tuition but we really weren't happy with the pressure she felt when working at history or world studies. The subjects were way beyond her comprehension even though we knew it was a reasonable syllabus for an average sixteen-year-old. Personally I found it easier to discuss the general election or the Chernobyl disaster with the deaf juniors at work than I did with Rachel. Even though she was living through the events it was like talking about an alien subject with her. They might as well have occurred on a different planet. It all seemed so futile and unnecessary for Rachel to try to study these subjects at this stage in her life: we felt as frustrated as she did.

Whole weekends and every evening were given over to homework to make sure she kept up to date with all the assignments and projects required for her courses, which we felt was too heavy a workload for her. Her history and world studies teachers both admitted that it was likely that she'd fail in those subjects so they did eventually agree to our request that Rachel should "drop" both subjects in order to concentrate on those in which she hoped to succeed. It was also agreed that she could have some work experience at a local nursery for handicapped children which not only gave her some relief from studying but also gave some support for her child care projects.

At fifteen years old Rachel was still naïve and immature but was beginning to show some independence away from the family unit. Although her language still remained a problem, she had now developed a few coping strategies of her own and would often simply "brush off" a conversation if she became muddled or tongue-tied.

Sometimes it would take her up to ten minutes to recall a word like "soup"; at other times she would say things like, "We're going to do a ballet dance in the next show". Now she'd been doing ballet dances since she was four years old but on that occasion she'd meant they would be doing a classical dance in tutus but couldn't find the words to explain it. She still often muddled things like similar road names such as East Street and Eastham Road which would cause her problems at times when going about the town independently.

In general her language was basic but adequate as she tended to speak in simple sentences but she always had problems when she wanted to explain something specific. Her understanding was also adequate for general life but she was out of her depth in school unless she could relate the subject to her own experiences or the subject was supported either visually or practically.

In her written work she always seemed to answer questions with a simple sentence when at least half a page or a paragraph was required. I remember one incident in cookery when she was asked to write a short essay on why she had chosen to cook a certain menu, for which she had already scored an A in the practical section. She submitted her answer in one sentence: "I chose these foods because they are good for you". Hardly sufficient for a GCSE pass!

Even after she had worked on a class lesson, repeated it with her private tutor and then spent more time at home with our support she would still hand in a one page essay full of grammatical errors, with full stops and capital letters scattered haphazardly all over the place, spelling errors and sometimes incomprehensible gibberish!

Chapter Ten
Diagnosis and Recognition

In the February before Rachel took her GCSEs we were offered an appointment at Guy's Hospital in the Newcomen Centre, which we gladly accepted. We went along at the appointed time and were seen by a paediatrician, clinical psychologist and a speech therapist who all asked Rachel questions about her work at school and what she thought was difficult in subjects like needlework, to which she replied, "I find the patterns difficult". I felt we were being patronised again when one of them said he thought everyone found those a little difficult to sort out at times! After about twenty minutes of general chat we were told that they didn't think Rachel had any major problems and that we could go. We both came out feeling extremely angry and frustrated, especially Rachel who cried because she felt they hadn't really believed in her. We'd hoped for so much at that appointment and came away with nothing yet again.

After a few weeks I was surprised to receive a letter from Pamela Moore, the Chief Speech Therapist at Guy's Hospital, who said she would be interested in seeing Rachel herself and offered us another appointment at the centre at the end of May. Obviously we agreed to go but Phil and I were puzzled by this strange turn of events. Apparently, although the other two doctors weren't interested in Rachel, the speech therapist must have thought something might be worth investigating.

We set off in good time to travel by train from the south coast to London, expecting to arrive with half an hour to spare, plenty of time to walk across the road from the station to the hospital. Unfortunately there was a problem on the line and we were stuck just outside the station for over three-quarters of an hour, and ended up running into the centre about twenty-five minutes late!

Essay on Schools

The schools were very different 100 years ago to what they are now.

Lessons were conducted in a different way. they had object lessons which were asking Questions about a certain object. The children when asked a question all answered together. This is parrot fashion. Parrot fashion is when everybody answers the question together for instance The teacher may ask, What is the capital of france the children altogether will answer paris. If the child was asked this question on his/her own they might not be able to answer or if the child was asked what is 2×4 they would probably not be able to answer without going through the table.

If also the children never learnt as much because they only had one person teaching a whole group of them most of the time and although they had the older children teaching the younger ones sometimes.

Children only learnt a few lessons like History, Geography, English and Arithmetic and then only what the teacher knew, which was a limited amount, or only what was in the book. that the teachers were given. If the children gave a wrong answer to what the teacher had in the book then the teacher were completely thrown for what to say next.

At the School the condisions of the children were poor they were dirty and about two out of fifteen were well dressed with faces washed etc. their were also not very clean school. the children were all squashed together with about 60 to one class and the teachers had quite a lot of children of all ages together the boys on one side and girls on another.

The schools were quite strict as well they had to read from the Bible and learn it. the schools also had a cane. and if anyone did anything wrong they used to be hit with the cane.

Rachel wrote this to submit as a GCSE piece. Her mother has copied it exactly using her own errors, syntax, use of capital letters and punctuation.

Pamela was already available and waiting for us, so we were shown straight into her room at approximately three o'clock, when she began taking a detailed history of Rachel's general and language development. She then chatted to Rachel in a relaxed fashion to assess her conversational ability and explained the special TROG tests that she wanted to use. Rachel was quite relaxed, happy and co-operative but the tests seemed endless.

She was shown lots of pictures of everyday objects but couldn't always recall their names, so said things like 'skirt' for 'kilt', even though she had a kilt herself and knew the name, or "I can't remember" when shown something like a bracelet, but indicated with her hands what she would do with it such as put it on her wrist.

In the next test Rachel was shown sets of four pictures and asked to indicate the one Pamela was describing. At first these were easy like, "Show me the cat on the chair" but gradually became harder for her. When Pamela said things like, "Show me the cow *being chased* by the boy" Rachel pointed to the cow actually *chasing* the boy instead.

Next she was asked to repeat simple sentences which were graded to become more complex and was asked to say rhyming words to the words Pamela was saying. Rachel was told a simple story about a dog, consisting of eleven short sentences and was asked to retell it, but could only remember half of it and so it went on.

Lots of other tests followed involving her listening skills and rhythm ability. All the way through the testing, Pamela was asking Rachel how she felt and how she had coped with each test to see what strategies, if any, Rachel had employed, but eventually Pamela finished her very thorough examination and proceeded to explain how Rachel had scored on all the various tests.

She said it was obvious that Rachel had in fact got a very specific language disorder, which she had learnt to live with, to some extent, by developing her own little coping strategies. Pamela went on to say that Rachel's ability at sixteen years of age was comparable with that of a twelve- to fourteen-year-old and that her problems were in both understanding language and in using it herself. Apparently her main problem areas were in mentally sorting out what was being said to her, grammar, sequencing words, understanding their meanings and recalling them to use herself. When I asked her about the cause of such a disorder she explained that the cause of language disorders was still unknown.

Pamela gave us some advice on how to improve Rachel's coping strategies and as we were planning to move to Cornwall after Rachel had finished school in July, she said she would write to the head of the speech therapy department in Plymouth to ask for some therapy sessions to be arranged as we would soon be in their health authority district. Pamela also recommended that we considered getting Rachel statemented by the education department to ensure that she had all the necessary help needed if she was to go on to college. Pamela then remarked upon the immense amount of effort that Rachel had shown in order to do the tests to the best of her ability and said that Rachel should definitely have been assessed and probably have attended a special school for language-impaired children when she was four years old. As we were preparing to leave, Pamela told us that she was surprised at how well we had all managed over the years.

When we actually left her room it was nearly six o'clock! Everywhere was in darkness and Pamela had to unlock the main doors to let us out. What a difference to all our other experiences! Nobody had ever gone to so much trouble for us before. I had a multitude of mixed emotions but felt both humble and grateful towards Pamela for all her time, compassion and professional ability.

I also felt extremely confused, frustrated and angry about the situation we were now in, as it was only a few days since Rachel had taken her last GCSE exam and it had taken until *now* for us to obtain the diagnosis we'd been searching for since she'd been born! Consequently Rachel had struggled needlessly through mainstream education either being patronised or having her problems ignored most of the time. I think we both left Guy's Hospital with a whole variety of emotions.

Rachel was extremely drained and exhausted after the extensive testing but was relieved to have a proper diagnosis at last which gave her hope for the future. It also gave her some self-worth as nothing had upset her more than being thought 'thick' by other people, especially her teachers.

Many a time Rachel had come home and cried because someone hadn't understood her or her problems at school, or because she had been aware that they hadn't believed us when we'd tried to explain the situation on her behalf. She now had more self-respect.

I also felt relieved but somewhat vindictive towards some of the other professionals we had dealt with in the past. When we arrived home and told Phil he felt just as frustrated and angry because of all the unnecessary suffering and struggling that Rachel had endured over the years. It seemed unbelievable to us that the special school Pamela had mentioned as being best for Rachel was only twelve miles away from our home, and I kept on thinking about how we had been patronised by most of the teachers she'd met in the mainstream system. It took me a long time to come to terms with the needless humiliation that Rachel had coped with and the fact that we had chosen to let Kevin Brown do her original assessment when she was six years old instead of my old friend Julie, a competent speech therapist who had just finished teaching at the local school for language-impaired children. I felt guilty because we had obviously made the wrong decision all those years ago and could have made Rachel's life a lot easier if only we'd let Julie do some tests, but in the end I rationalised with myself by realising that Rachel was probably a stronger person as a result of her experiences. She was certainly very sensitive towards other people's feelings and needs, which was probably due to her own struggles and emotional battles over the years, and at least we'd been given the strength and ability to cope with her problems.

The biggest difficulty now was to get her diagnosis accepted by the education system and to try again for college. Knowing that we would be moving to Liskeard, just over the Cornish border, as soon as she had finished school, Rachel had applied to NNEB college courses in both Plymouth and Cornwall, but thanks to the letter sent from her senior school, written by the new head of house teacher who had never even taught Rachel, Cornwall had refused to give her an interview. I think I will always remember the day that letter arrived. Rachel picked it up and opened it excitedly, having seen the postmark, expecting to be offered an interview date, but instead she was devastated when she read that in view of the letter sent from her school it didn't really seem worthwhile interviewing her. Rachel was heartbroken but I was angry to think that anyone could be judged in such a way and not be given a chance to prove oneself to be worthy of consideration.

Phil and I decided to do our best to make them reconsider their decision, so we rallied around and sent off references from her private tutors, employers, Guiders and even her Guide Commissioner who had always admired Rachel's fortitude, and various other people who had seen her working with children, along with an explanatory letter from us and a request for them to review her application. After that,

Cornwall did agree to see her and Plymouth was automatically willing to interview her as they had various levels of child care courses available to students, but Rachel was adamant that she would only accept NNEB at this stage. Unfortunately she failed to be accepted by either college but she was able to accept that, as she knew it was due to her own merits and debits and not as the result of a letter of condemnation from the school – although it must obviously have had a lot of influence on the colleges. Rachel therefore applied to go into the sixth form at Liskeard School for one year, where she was accepted, and planned to reapply for an NNEB course the following year.

I spent many, many hours on the telephone trying to initiate Rachel's statementing, but West Sussex didn't want to know about her as she was now sixteen years old, even though statementing was valid until a student was nineteen years of age. Obviously Cornwall couldn't initiate things until after she had entered one of their schools. I'm afraid I didn't know then that I could have demanded she was statemented and initiated the process myself! One thing I did manage to arrange whilst still in West Sussex was an overview with the careers adviser for the handicapped in order to have some information about Rachel's rights should she fail to achieve her aim once we were in Cornwall.

I also spoke to the head of the only senior school for the language-impaired in the country, to ask for his advice on how to get Rachel into college. He thought she should be exempt from the entrance exams and that statementing was essential. The head of the AFASIC Association in London said the same thing but I was unable to obtain any satisfactory responses from County Hall.

That summer we moved to Cornwall and in August Rachel received her GCSE results which we felt were surprisingly good and reflected all the hard work she'd done. Her worst subject was maths, which was no surprise, for which she had an F, and she had an E in home economics which was probably due to the problems she'd had with the theory and nutrition section. We were pleased to learn that she had passed her typing exams and had a D in needlework, but were amazed to find she had another D for English, which was probably due to all her private tuition, but best of all was her C in child care!

A week before school was due to start we were all invited to look around the sixth form section and meet the head of the department. He was kind, showed interest in Rachel's problems and asked for a copy of the Guy's Hospital report. The different attitude in Cornwall compared with West Sussex was something we were soon to get used to and for which we were immensely grateful. In fact I began to lose count of all the copies of that report that were sent out in various directions for different people's files. It was wonderfully reassuring to see how everything just seemed to fall into place.

Rachel began her speech therapy sessions in a building near the school, at nine o'clock in the morning once a week, but I went with her for the first session to give her moral support. As I thought she was old enough to attend such sessions by herself, I let her go alone for the next one but was disappointed to find that she had forgotten to attend but had gone into school instead as usual. We encouraged her to make her own apologies and confirm the next appointment, which she did, but subsequently forgot that appointment as well, even though she'd been reminded of where to go when we'd said "Goodbye". This was so typical of her that we decided to let the people who were trying to help her see how she performed normally. We felt there was no point in masking her problems by helping her to avoid them in this situation. We insisted that Rachel should make her own arrangements again but she took so many days in doing so that I secretly phoned her speech therapist to explain what had happened.

In the meantime we had been sent an appointment for a school medical, which we assumed was routine for all new school entrants, but it was obviously due to the good communication between various departments as we discovered when the doctor said she'd heard that Rachel had missed two speech therapy appointments. She asked what the problem had been and on learning of Rachel's difficulties suggested that the appointments were changed to 9.15 a.m. so that Rachel wouldn't follow the flow into school but be more likely to follow the intended course. This was arranged and subsequently worked well with Rachel successfully attending the planned sessions and so learning the new strategies to compensate for her problems.

We were also impressed by the fact that during the first half term, we had not only met all her teachers on her new course who were all wanting to bend over backwards to help her, but had also met many other people who would be involved in her education that year. Phil and I were invited to one meeting with the head of the remedial department and the educational psychologist when we all sat around a table to discuss the Guy's Hospital report together and how they envisaged helping Rachel to succeed in the next year by ensuring a place at the local college. Both these ladies had an amazing amount of empathy and understanding. They also had a wonderful commitment to their work and we couldn't have wished for better support. For the first time in Rachel's life I felt I could leave it all to the professionals to deal with and felt confident that they wouldn't let us down. Appointments were made for both of them to meet Rachel individually in the following week, after which all the cogs seemed to spring into action and be turning satisfactorily. As the help available was so personally geared to Rachel's needs we didn't feel there was any need to pursue the statementing issue now that we were in Cornwall but decided to watch closely and be prepared to jump into action should the need arise – but it never did.

There was still one more offer of help which endeared us to all these caring people and that was when Rachel's new English teacher came to our house to ask how he could best help Rachel improve her English grade in case she needed a C pass to enter college. He was willing to give her extra coaching in a lunch hour and made her promise to see him at any break time should she feel unsure about the class work. There were other offers and recommendations too for further coaching and special concessions but Rachel had all she needed and wanted to build up a normal relationship with her new peers so we gratefully declined on her behalf. During that year Rachel not only improved in confidence but also academically and socially, so much so, that she actually won a place at the local college for the next NNEB course on her own merits! It had been agreed that she would be exempt from the entrance exam in as much as she would not be judged on the marks, but they asked her to sit it along with the other applicants to give them an idea of her ability. She passed with sixty-four per cent!

Rachel also gained successful passes in her school subjects as she managed to go up a grade to E in maths. She maintained a D grade in English and in business studies but surprised us by gaining a D grade in geography which she had previously found too difficult to cope with as a GCSE subject. Her best pass was a C in social studies, which amazed us all, considering it had been the accompanying subject dropped from her old GCSE syllabus. She also passed stage one in office practice and gained the CPVE certificates. Everything looked set for the future and we were very proud of her.

Chapter Eleven

The Chance of a Future

Rachel entered college in September 1989 along with about eighteen other girls aged between sixteen and twenty-five years of age. She immediately gelled with a group of three other girls, developing a special relationship with one of them which is still in existence today.

Although she was never actually statemented, Rachel's two main tutors did ask for a copy of the Guy's Hospital report and asked their educational psychologist to make a further assessment and report. Surprisingly, this happened to be the same lady who had first seen Rachel after her arrival in Liskeard School and her three-page report proved to be invaluable. She said that Rachel was of good intelligence but was slow at processing her thoughts due to sequencing problems but not due to any lack of intellectual ability. She said that Rachel had a good vocabulary but suffered from word finding problems. Rachel's test results were very varied as she was able to use some well-developed strategies in some tests, whereas in others, although she had given the right answer she had exceeded the time limit so the score was invalid.

It was also noted that Rachel had obvious difficulty when she had to reorganise information in her memory, as required when doing mathematics, but that she performed much better with multiple choice-type questions. She displayed no reading problems but her spelling was weak for her age due to the sequencing problems, but her errors were only minor so it was always clear to the reader what she intended to write.

The report concluded that Rachel had all the necessary skills in reading, writing and spelling for the course and that the examining process should be within her capabilities. The part that the psychologist had difficulty in commenting upon was Rachel's internal thought processes which were needed to retrieve information from her memory, organise, plan and write an answer in response to a question. She said that this process would take Rachel a long time and would be hampered by tiredness or stress. She even said that she had been aware of Rachel taking a long time to consider her responses before answering a question in general conversation.

On reflection, after reading that report, I was reminded of the comments made by one of Rachel's junior school teachers after he had watched her do a multiple choice paper, and he had remarked upon her slow thought processes. Unfortunately Rachel's problems were not being acknowledged in those days, but he must have been a very perceptive man.

The college sent both reports on Rachel to the NNEB board asking for extra time and any other suitable allowances to be made for such things as poor spelling. The result was that Rachel would only be judged on the content of the answers providing that the examiners could clearly understand what she meant. The college also decided that Rachel should sit some mock exams at the end of the first year along with the final students in order to familiarise her with the setting. The marks were not recorded but her tutors went over each paper with her and used the information gained to improve Rachel's skills during the last year. Again we felt satisfied that we couldn't ask for more, so we left the situation in the hands of these obviously caring and experienced people.

Rachel enjoyed college and coped remarkably well, especially with all the practical work on her various placements, although she did suffer from extreme anxiety at times when travelling alone on a new route for the first time, or when she was unsure of what would be expected of her in a new setting. However, her usual determination and fortitude saw her through such situations. Her main problems lay in keeping up with all the projects and assignments, and Rachel's tutors were aware that she needed some support from us. However, they said that was acceptable, as all students obtained information from a variety of resources and that they would be able to monitor Rachel's ability by the essays produced in college. She was also allowed to use the word processor at home that we had bought her, which proved a great asset as she didn't have to rewrite all her work several times before handing it in.

Nevertheless there were times when I would sit up in bed, late at night, to read through a book for her, making notes of all the relevant pages and paragraphs so that she could make a quicker start in writing up an essay. At other times when she was tired, she would lie in bed and tell me the facts she wanted written. I would then write them all down for her with correct grammar and spelling so that she could copy it out the next day. Even with the word processor she needed help at times in organising the presentation of a project or in extending one of her – all too brief – answers on an assignment or placement that she had done. There were also many occasions when Phil would be involved as well, as we worked our way through brochures, leaflets and magazines, cutting out suitable pictures to illustrate her work so that she could reach her deadline.

Rachel did not want to make use of her concession of extra time if she could avoid it, as she preferred to be treated the same as the other students, which we respected. Only once did she need to ask for extra time when a project was handed in two days late.

At the end of the exhausting but enjoyable two years, Rachel sat the examination alongside her peers. It seemed strange afterwards not to have the pressure of another assignment hanging over all our heads. We now had nothing to do but await the results with bated breath.

One of the ironic things to happen was that Rachel was the first one on her course to secure a full-time post. She had been working for a family in the holidays with a four-year-old boy who was severely handicapped by cerebral palsy and asthma, but the family now felt they required a full-time, live-in nanny. Rachel was their first choice as she already knew the child and how to cope with all his special needs and she was glad to accept, especially as she would be involved with learning the Hungarian (Peto) type of physiotherapy in which she was interested. We were also relieved, as not only would she be spared the trauma of interviews until she was more confident and mature, but we thought it would relieve some of the pressure hanging over her during the examination period.

Rachel settled into her new regime extremely well soon after leaving college, and everyone who knew her was amazed at the newly found confidence that she began to display.

Early in August the long-awaited envelope arrived on our hall floor containing her examination results. As they arrived a few days earlier than expected I didn't know what was inside, so simply placed it on the Welsh dresser ready to give to her when she came home. Later that day Rachel telephoned to say that she'd heard from a friend that the results had been released, so asked if an envelope had arrived and would we open it for her. Suddenly the moment of truth had arrived, and I felt very confused. I had always felt confident that she would cope with the course but now I began to wonder if we had really done the right thing by encouraging her to aim so high. Would we have to tell her she'd failed? I desperately prayed not. Surely life couldn't be so cruel. She had worked so hard and come so far, surely only success could follow now. I'd had complete faith in her up until that moment but suddenly I was full of doubt and felt guilty in case Rachel should receive yet another knock in life.

As all those thoughts flashed through my mind I found I couldn't bring myself to open the envelope so gave it to Phil and waited while he did the ominous deed. Time seemed to stand still for the few seconds it took him to look at the card and read out the result. *She had passed!* I just can't describe the mixed feelings of relief and joy that swept over me at that moment. I found it hard to believe that all those years of struggling and fighting for Rachel were actually over! Had we really reached our goal at last? It seemed like a dream but there we all were – awake and talking together on the telephone.

After telling Rachel the good news we said that we would take the card straight round to her house so that she could see it for herself. Then Phil and I just stood there and hugged each other for some minutes, after which I began to cry. It was as though all the pent-up emotions of the last few years were flowing out of me. Rachel had realised her dream at last. She had always wanted to do the NNEB course, which she had completed – but now she had passed their examination as well! I was so proud of her. I felt as ecstatic as though I'd just had a child pass out of Oxford or Cambridge with honours. To us it was just as great an achievement, and I wanted to tell the world about it!

When we arrived at Rachel's new home we all hugged each other and cried. Even her new boss joined in and offered us all a glass of wine to celebrate the event. She then told Rachel that she was to have the evening off to accompany us to a party to celebrate properly.

Following Rachel's success at college we were even prouder to learn that they had now decided to take on other students with similar problems; the first one being a dyslexic student on the very next course.

It seemed a fitting end to all our struggles and was good to know that our battle had not only proved worthwhile to Rachel but had also opened the door for others.

Appendix I
Battleground Strategies and Helpful Hints for Parents

In order to cope with Rachel's screaming and frustration tantrums I found it best to try to 'switch off' emotionally. This was not always easy to do, especially in the early days, but eventually I was able to think, "Here we go again!" and go through the motions of rocking her and waiting until she could be reasoned with. I repeat it is much easier said than done but it is much better to stay in control of the situation rather than join in. When a child is so upset because it is frightened or confused it needs someone to give it security – the last thing it will need is for you to 'crack up' as well.

When teaching Rachel we found that everything had to be taught through touch or experience. We had to use as much practical apparatus as we could find to teach her anything, which was why the toy library proved so useful and Phil made the counting rods and cubes to teach her tens and units. Telling and showing her just didn't work. I refer to the old Chinese proverb:

> *Tell me and I forget*
> *Show me and I see*
> *Involve me and I remember.*

We actually taught Rachel to write correctly by using her index (pointing) finger to trace the shapes on rough surfaces and in sand. In this way the message reached her brain through the sense of touch, after which the pencil became an extension of her forefinger.

Children need lots of physical experience such as climbing, hopping and skipping in order to become well co-ordinated. Some people believe that the left and right patterning movement of crawling is an important preliminary exercise in learning to read and write.

Children need to be skilful in PE-type activities before they can control the finer movements needed for threading, cutting, colouring, tracing, drawing and finally writing.

Rachel also had to learn to control her hand and eye activities as the two just didn't seem to work together at all. We did this by throwing her a large beach ball at close range and slowly moving further away; gradually we began to use smaller balls and eventually we could use a bat and ball.

Many children who have learning difficulties have failed to develop a dominant side, as had Rachel. As she was basically right handed, we had to make her consciously aware of *always* using her right hand for pointing (including using the proper pointing finger), picking things up, etc.

To make Rachel use her right eye we encouraged her to spend about five minutes once or twice a day looking through a kaleidoscope, telescope or some sort of peep-hole activity.

To make Rachel right-footed we taught her to play hopscotch, always hopping on the right foot and encouraged this to be played as often as seemed reasonable, even when walking down the street by using the paving slab patterns. Some children may prefer practising kicking a ball with their appropriate foot.

Dancing also helped Rachel to have better co-ordination and become more aware of her left and right sides. The repeated practising and sequencing of movement proved an added bonus in helping her to train her memory.

Some children have problems in school due to chronic ear conditions which cause fluctuating hearing problems. It is always worthwhile keeping a regular check on your child's hearing should you suspect this to be the case. Your family doctor or child's school nurse should be able to help you with this.

Some children who have reading and spelling difficulties are unable to focus easily on a word as they have difficulty in actually converging their eyes. This can be easily checked out and if necessary corrected by seeing an orthoptist, which again your family doctor or school nurse should be able to arrange.

Appendix II

The opening sentence of the 1989 Children Act says that "The welfare of the child is paramount", and goes on to say that parents have responsibilities towards their children to see that everything necessary for their child's welfare is carried out.

This obviously encourages parents to follow their rightful instincts to *fight* for their child should it be necessary, just as they would if they saw their child drowning!

All too often a caring parent feels inhibited and doesn't want to make a fuss – but my advice to parents who feel their child has a problem that is being ignored by a professional person is – *don't be afraid* to ask for a second opinion.

Doctors can refer your child to a variety of different specialists in many different departments where further investigations can be carried out or expert advice can be gained. This could also include the help of a speech and language therapist should you be worried about your child's language development.

Schools can refer your child to an educational psychologist to investigate whether it has any learning difficulties.

Statementing is a process whereby a child is fully examined physically, mentally and academically whenever there is concern regarding that child's education and can be initiated by parents, school or medical personnel. This procedure should take six months to complete but does sometimes take longer. When all the necessary information has been gathered together recommendations are made for the child's future educational needs, which the education system is then obliged to follow. Parents are involved in the process and have the right to appeal against the final decision should they wish to do so. Statements are reviewed annually.

The current Education Act and Children Act should be available for anyone to read at local libraries. In some cases it is also available in simplified layman's terms.

Some Useful Phone Numbers and Addresses

For free advice on education, statementing and related legal matters:
ACE (Advisory Centre for Education), 1b Aberdeen Studios, 22-24 Highbury Grove, London N5 2EA. Tel: 071-354 8321 (2-5 p.m.).
Children's Legal Centre, 20 Compton Terrace, London N1 2UN. Tel: 071-359 6251 (2-5 p.m.).
IPSEA (Independent Panel of Special Education Advisers), 12 Marsh Road, Tillingham, Essex, CM0 7SZ. Tel: 0621 779781.

For information on claiming benefits (e.g. attendance allowance):
Network for the Handicapped Ltd., Bedford House, 35 Emerald Street, London WC1N 3QL. Tel: 071-831 8031 (Contact: Helen Berent).

For information on speech and language disorders:
AFASIC (Association For All Speech Impaired Children), 347 Central Markets, Smithfield, London EC1A 9NH. Tel: 071-236 3632/6487.

For information on special schools, language units, etc.:
ICAN (Invalid Children's Aid Nationwide), 10 Bowling Green Lane, Farringdon, London EC1R 0BD.

N.B. Your Local Education Authority should be able to give you details of provision in your area.